Under a Covid Skye

UNDER A COVID SKYE

*An island year through columns
from the West Highland Free Press*

by John White

Published in 2024 by Linicro Press, Isle of Skye
www.linicropress.co.uk • books@linicropress.co.uk

© John White 2024

The moral right of John White to be identified as
the author of this work has been asserted in accordance
with the Copyright, Designs & Patents Act 1988.

Printed by Imprint Digital, UK

Book design by Lumphanan Press
www.lumphananpress.co.uk

ISBN: 978-1-7384169-0-5

Foreword • 9

Introduction • 11

Chapter One • 15
March to April 2020

Chapter Two • 39
May to June 2020

Chapter Three • 83
July to August 2020

Chapter Four • 131
September to October 2020

Chapter Five • 179
November to December 2020

Chapter Six • 219
January to February 2021

Acknowledgments • 277

For Anne, Talitha and Rònan

Foreword

Since he joined us in 2020, John White has proven to be an excellent addition to the West Highland Free Press team, with his thoughtful and topical columns every Thursday.

Like all good columnists there is plenty of variety in his work – with John touching on a whole host of issues, from Covid to cancer; music and travel; nature, education, energy and community.

Though he doesn't shy away from difficult subjects, he doesn't lecture or pontificate and there is always reason and perspective in his words.

His columns reveal much about his own life – from his upbringing in the north of England, to travels in the middle east, his career as an outdoor instructor and family life with Anne and the kids at home in north Skye. All of those adventures give John a good sense of the global and the local, but while his writing often draws on personal experience, it is never self-indulgent.

It is hard to find many positives from the Covid-enforced lockdowns of 2020, but as far as our newspaper was concerned one undoubted boost arrived when John decided he would try his hand at writing a column.

During that awful spring one subject dominated all of our minds, and John had taken to writing in a bid to make some sense of it. He may have seen the idea as initially therapeutic but it was to prove a gift to the newspaper.

I am delighted he has compiled his columns in this book, and hope that his work (which I should add always arrives on time and to the correct word count!) will continue to grace the pages of our newspaper long into the future,

Keith MacKenzie
Editor, West Highland Free Press

Introduction

It is a privilege to have a weekly column published in a newspaper, a thousand or so words about anything I want, printed, to be hopefully read by at least some of the paper's purchasers.

When the West Highland Free Press returned to print after the first lockdown, I wrote about the importance of journalism, but also the irony of opinion being cheap. I tell stories based on some semblance of fact or real experience, but they are really a carrot to my opinion. A friend joked about there being a weekly message, which concerned me a little, and I worried if some weeks they might read more like a sermon. Ministerial I am certainly not.

When writing I sometimes imagine people I know. Visualising a readership helps me engage, whilst perhaps trying to nudge thoughts and opinions. I try never to antagonise, believing it counterproductive in both argument as well as life, but I strive to write in a reasoned rational way. Even if people disagree with my opinion, they might hopefully appreciate my point of view.

If I have a technique then it is to recount a tale, a story whether mine or taken from other sources, leading into a narrative which is hopefully relevant. I try to be current, appropriate, perhaps global in theme, sometimes local, sometimes personal, often all three. I feel it is appropriate to be honest and give a little of the life I have experienced,

There is also of course the pandemic, a unique time which obviously gets regular treatment. My first piece was a personal reaction to the unfolding events. The columns grew from that first article, I basically just didn't stop writing, and my musings seemed to hit a chord locally. I have to recognise that the columns, and therefore this book, would have never come to fruition without Covid and its effect, it is both a theme and a reason.

The columns are a personal snapshot of an unprecedented time. It is perhaps unique in that they were written during the uncertainty of that time, no retrospection, no hindsight. There are real fears, real anxieties, and real hopes. Covid on Skye.

But I have also written about immortal jellyfish and delivering prescriptions on my Ducati motorbike, I have written about being on mountain in a whiteout, and the starlings at my bird feeder. I have written about art and cutting logs.

The stories are varied and can come from a five minute encounter, a brief experience, or the condensing of a lengthy adventure. Books I have read, films watched can all be inspiration or material, as can radio interviews. Social media can highlight an issue, even if producing the inevitable polarisation of opinion, which I try to rationalise.

Some are more light-hearted than others, some were difficult to write, some I am particularly proud of. My wife

Anne occasionally keeps me right, proofreading them all before I 'file' them. Occasionally she gets me to be more sensitive or will suggest a different word here or there. Sometimes she accuses me of obfuscation, so I simplify things.

Like many involved in the tourist industry, I do a lot of cleaning. Vacuuming floors is therapeutic and doubles up as column thinking time. I often go over sentences and ideas in my head while polishing shower screens.

West Highland Free Press editor Keith Mackenzie writes the headers for each column and so each week when I get the paper, I turn to see if he takes the same angle that I intended. He nearly always does; I have used his titles for each article.

If there is ever a message as my friend suggested, couched in the theme of a story, it is of understanding, respect, and compassion.

J.W., Isle of Skye, 2023

Chapter One

March to April 2020

Covid 19 and life on Skye – from denial to realisation / Fluctuating between normality and despondency / Zoom yoga and the empty wide-open spaces of Skye / We must celebrate the life we have / As the air clears, we can re-evaluate what is essential in our lives

(On 25th April the WHFP ceased to print, but continued with an online presence)

Friday 27th March

Covid 19 and life on Skye – from denial to realisation

As Anne and I were listening to Nicola Sturgeon being interviewed on Radio Scotland this morning, I felt like we were in a movie, sat huddled around the wireless as if listening to Neville Chamberlain's declaration of war, gleaning information from the radio, and trying to assess the impact of a new normality and the encroachment of significant life-changing behaviour.

Despite running a tourist, education, and entertainment business on Skye, that like all, had first huge cancellations, eventually followed by our own decision to shut up shop for the foreseeable future, despite the prospect of probably little or no income for the next, well maybe few months, I think I was in some kind of denial.

On the first cancellation, I threw the booking sheet in the wastepaper basket, but after the next three came in, I rescued the sheet, flattened it out and began filing them. These were only accommodation bookings. Then the schools and youth groups for the outdoor centre cancelled, big bookings. The leadership centre Columba 1400 who we work closely with and provides us with a regular weekly booking, closed. The file of cancellations is thick, but I haven't bothered adding up the money lost, knowing won't help.

Anne decided to cancel a recording trip to India and a couple of days later India stopped allowing travel, her new CD will be delayed indefinitely. Her tutoring work in schools went the same way. There is a possibility that she could do some of her facilitation work via video conferencing, so we have fingers crossed for that, and she might help transpose and develop residential experiences to online at-home resources.

But still it felt academic. We have savings, the money put aside for the CD development can be spent on the mortgage and food. I had planned some biggish work on the centre, that money we can use for the bills. The fat from the last couple of years of tourism bounty is a buffer. I know that there are many who are not in such a fortunate position...

We decided to embrace social distancing, but still enjoy walking the hills, and ticked off a couple more trig points from Ian Stewart and Alistair Christie's walking guidebook.[1]

But as containment moved to the 'flattening of the curve' and as a population we started to understand more about projections and modelling and statistics there was a creeping realisation, this is a real crisis.

It was only when I married up the economic and impact on our business to actual real health issues, and the fact that people will die, that things began to sink in.

I think the denial was finally put to bed when I realised

---

1. Christie, A. and Stewart, I. *Trig Point Walks on the Isle of Skye and Raasay* (2014) Isle of Skye. Strupag Publications.

I wanted my family home, I wanted my children with me... My daughter is living in Edinburgh, doing a degree, her exams were cancelled and lectures stopped. She was meant to go to Cairo for an intensive language course... she decided not to go, a few days before travel there was ceased... My son is at college in Galashiels on a sports performance course. His downhill mountain bike races have been cancelled... this was going to be his year, he has trained all winter, was aiming for podiums in the early Scottish races, and had a hope of gaining 'a jersey' maybe riding for Britain in a world cup. Disappointments, I think I was as 'gutted' as he, but perspective slowly realised. The First Minister said teenagers may feel that they are invincible and may see school and college closures as a welcome holiday, but they can pass on the virus even if it affects them less, and if they enjoy an extreme sport, any accident will just add to the NHS burden.

My kids are living their lives in their flats, but as a parent of course I worry, I want them home, that natural instinct to protect. I have brought my kids up to be independent and self-sufficient, but in my head that all goes out the window... they are still my children... still children.

I have suggested that they at least keep the vehicles full of fuel so they can get home in one go if they need to. I think a tankful should suffice and if the Highlands is shut to stop visitors, make sure they can prove residency here.

Crisis brings out the best and worst in people, and social media is both a lifeline for some in isolation, but also the peddler of false information and a hotbed of irrational radicalism. I would urge people to be careful what they write, avoid inflammatory and unhelpful comments. If there is a desire to say something, say it with compassion.

On the positive side we can Skype, video conference and have virtual cèilidhs. A friend Hamish Napier was due to launch his latest album, but the tour was cancelled. Instead, a live stream release. His mother and father sat with him (dressed up in tuxedos and hats) they played the album, and we commented on messenger. Hamish sat and chatted and welcomed people as they commented, drams were had and more importantly so was craic.

I don't even want to mention the negativity that exists on social media, most of it stems from fear and ignorance rather than malice, but as we try to evoke some wartime blitz spirit to get through this crisis, remember the Second World War saw a huge rise in crime, theft, murders, and conning. I believe that good will always prevail, but we must be aware of those that desire to take an immoral advantage from a situation.

My favourite Covid 19 joke has been, 'If I need to quarantine with my husband, it won't be the virus that kills him', but I am mindful that for many, especially socially disadvantaged and socially vulnerable, the home environment is not perhaps a safe place. There are people who live in abusive and dysfunctional situations. For them social isolation may be a sentence that is unrealistic. People may still need to wander the streets...

I however will paint my buildings until the paint runs out, I made oatcakes for the first-time last night, if I can get some yeast I am going to brew some beer. I am going to write more, Skype my friends and family, do more yoga and become a better fiddle player. I will also walk the hills, but the less visited ones and only with Anne. I am relishing spending more quality time with her.

These are unprecedented times, a phrase that may seem dramatic and overused, but compassion and kindness will pull us through.

Friday 3rd April

Fluctuating between normality and despondency

Last Thursday at eight o'clock, like many, I went out to applaud the NHS 'frontline' staff. The evening was spectacular, a fingernail moon was outshone by Venus and the stars were coming out, a post-sunset glow filled the lower half of the sky, and there wasn't a breath of wind. It was too beautiful to make a noise as nature was doing its own job. The amazing sound of drumming snipe filled the air. That weird and wonderful sound of spring and early summer is made by the bird's tail feathers vibrating as it drops from high up, males showing off to females of course. This natural rhythm perhaps applause enough for humanity...

The next morning, one of my friends, a doctor thanked people on his Facebook, but reposted an angry comment from another doctor asking what people were doing at the last ballot box and how did they allow the NHS to get into such a sorry state, before this situation. This is not the time for politicising the crisis, but when it is all over and we enter a new normal, a new reality, perhaps society will have re-examined its values. There was a fabulous song doing the rounds by Jeffery Lewis a line of which went; 'Old ways will freeze, and we'll have new priorities'.

Life in lockdown. I have to confess to being all over the place, fluctuating between normality and despondency. Sleep patterns seem muddled, some nights I lie awake, a sure sign of anxiety whilst other nights I am fine and snore away for a good few hours. The following days, the 'mojo' and attitude reflect this. I'm possibly drinking the odd beer more than normal so I must keep an eye on that.

But there is work to do. Those in the North end will have noticed our wind turbine has gone from the landscape. A few weeks ago it seized up, and now I have had the time to lower it and investigate the problem.

That was a good day, getting on with stuff, life going on as normal, fixing and sorting which is what many of us do in this rural Highland way, working from home anyway. In some respect, I almost feel guilty, embracing the isolation and the distancing, and enjoying having different routines to work to. But I don't live in a Glasgow tenement with 3 kids under 12 with home schooling and home working issues. I can get outside easily whenever I want. I can exercise on the croft for more than an hour a day.

The government seems to be coming through with financial support, of course it will take a bit of time, and the inevitable gaps which people fall through will have to be caulked, perhaps and hopefully by a Universal Basic Income, but the self-employed who haven't been operating long enough, and those between jobs will need to be supported somehow. I am intrigued that amounts to be awarded seem to be considerably higher than most traditional benefits within the welfare state. Perhaps when it is all over there will a paradigm shift in attitudes to the requirements of those out of work and in need, because for a while we were all in need. We are all 'benefit scroungers' now.

On the days when I struggle and can't seem to get anything done my mind flits from one thing to another, there is a lack of concentration perhaps due to lack of sleep, and the anxiety. Will the money come through? Will tourists ever come back? Have I caught the virus?

Will any of my friends or family die?

And then there is the endless media and social media discussion... wall-to-wall Covid cover, my word, it is all we can talk about. It is incessant, continual constant conversation. On one hand like a torture of white noise, on the other a necessary communication of events and developments. The house becomes like a pressure cooker of opinion, false expertise and discussion. Occasionally I feel the need to ban social media and the radio. 'Hello, my name is John and I haven't spoken about Corona for... well 5 minutes.'

And the waiting... we are just waiting because we don't know how it will pan out.

I find the waiting the hardest.

Channel 4 news were on the Island, some journalists are seen as key workers. People need news to help them through, and that news needs to be gathered. They wanted to film Anne (from a distance...!) singing from the decking, I suppose in the spirit of the Italian balcony. A couple of hours before they came we got the message their accommodation had been cancelled and they had nowhere to stay. They had tents just in case but that would seem worse. Of course, they stayed in two of our wigwam cabins, and the Skye foodbank got an appropriate donation from them. I could not take money, we are closed and I cannot profit from a crisis.

As Anne sang you could see this hardened experienced journalist who reports from all over the world was moved... Music does that, and music is doing its thing to help us through, there is a wonderful Gaelic proverb, 'mairidh gaol is ceòl.'

Duncan Chisolm the fiddler, has started #Covidcèilidh and each day he plays a tune and posts it on social media. People are encouraged to do similar, His first tune was 'Maidhdeannan na h-airigh' a song which Anne sings, and one of my favourites. I have decided to learn it, a slow air. Well, they are really more difficult than faster tunes because you can hear every squeak and scratch, but I am getting there, and maybe soon, I will inflict the internet with a version. Bruce Macgregor, another fiddler, is running 5 o'clock sessions and hopes to gather together a body of favourite session tunes. His first set had Jenny Dang the Weaver... I intend to be able to play that in the sessions in the Ferry Inn, the Glenfinnan Hotel, The Old Inn at Carbost and the Edinbane Inn when we can begin again.

Haud me back...

'Love and music will endure.'

Friday 10th April

Zoom Yoga and the empty wide open spaces of Skye

A big disappointment of the week was the postponement of Runrig streaming the film of their last concert in 2018. It seems ironic that a virtual event has been put off, but apparently there are 'problematic copyright algorithms...!'

'The Last Dance' was quite simply an amazing experience, and in years to come it will probably attain 'bragging rights' status and people will say 'I was there' ... We were.

The band played their hearts out, but none more so than Malcolm Jones, performing like we had never heard before, more riffs and solos with nods to the odd rock cover.

We danced and sang, played our part in the choruses and classics, waved our arms, chanted the anthems and wiped a tear away when it was all over. Reliving it, albeit on a screen will be a treat, and at the moment we need treats.

Both Anne and I are spending a lot of time on devices, but in newfound ways. Three weeks ago, nobody had heard of Zoom, but now everybody is at it (other videoing conference platforms are available...!) I took part in a virtual SEALL (Skye Events For All) board meeting. where we discussed the efforts being made to survive the crisis. Feis an Eilean, the Island Festival is of course being cancelled, and we have to cross our fingers for the Festival of Small Halls due to run in November.

A friend who works in the arts in Edinburgh told me someone has coined the phrase 'unproducing'. Events concerts and festivals which at this time of year are usually being busily put together, are instead being postponed and unorganised. Teams are trying to work out ways of continuing their existence, moving forward while staying at home.

Counteracting this, artists and musicians are being productive, as more and more things are happening from front rooms and kitchens. I wonder how long this creative outburst will last, I hope it is sustainable as the novelty of lockdown wears off.

With Zoom, you get a meeting invitation from the host, and after clicking on a link and spending the first few moments discussing blank screens and muted microphones and the fact that somebody might be in their pyjamas... then you have an effective way of having contact, for business or pleasure. Simon at Earth and Skye Yoga in Staffin has run Zoom yoga sessions successfully with about 12 of us and Anne has had a conference with over 20 people. As a family we managed a real game of Scrabble with our daughter in Leith, using Facetime for her to see her letters and Zoom to see the board. This family contact is crucial especially for people living alone, especially as the days turn to weeks and very possibly to months.

I heard a priest on the radio suggest that social distancing is an unhelpful phrase. Whilst physically distancing ourselves, we can still be social. Technology allows this, and luddites the county over are embracing it.

We still have occasional face-to-face conversation. When in the garden and people walk by on their daily exercise, we can talk while keeping a safe distance and a fence between us.

And people are walking, I am seeing many more people pass the house, one set of neighbours stride past at the same time every day, saying ironically how nice it is with so few cars on the road. They used to walk to church on Sundays, but not in recent times due to the traffic... I have heard people say how a visit to Portree is like 20 years ago, and lockdown described like 'Sundays of old'

I am writing this on Monday morning, and by the time it is printed things might have changed, as developments unfold at speed. In the towns and cities there seem to be a number of people flouting the distancing recommendations, and as the sun comes out we have seen pictures of seemingly inappropriate picnics and sunbathing in urban public parks.

This reminds us as to how lucky we are living in this less populated and beautiful place. We can enjoy this empty landscape while staying close to home for our exercise. It is clear that the instructions from governments have an urban /suburban bias, but we still need to play our part. Humans need green space, need fresh air and the wind and sun (and rain) on their face. Many of us just need to walk out the front door to experience this, even those in the more built-up areas of our big villages/small towns are still no more than a few minutes' walk away from hills, shores and even trees. Imagine living in a small space with children and only a window looking out onto buildings from a few floors up, and not feeling you can go outside…

As the chief medical officer resigns for not following her own advice and driving an hour to a second home, we have to follow the mantra 'Stay home protect the NHS save lives' especially as our demographic is possibly more vulnerable than in other places. When it comes it might hit us hard.

I took my first trip to the Portree Co-Op in two weeks to be met by a cheery smile from a gatekeeper at the entrance, allowing one in to one out. The queue was not huge, but I tried to rattle round as quickly as possible to avoid people outside having to wait. Of course, this meant getting flustered and muddled, and taking longer than necessary. It was strange edging past people, giving knowing glances to friends and brief comments about the situation, a shake of the head rather than a long chat while blocking the fruit and veg aisle. Despite the real smiles from the staff, I found the experience a little unsettling, and was glad to get home. Perhaps social distancing and staying at home is causing the onset of a slight agoraphobia.

We now all know what furlough means. I wondered if the word had roots in agriculture, sounding like leaving a field fallow, lazybeds or feannagan. But it does just mean leave of absence. We have had to furlough our main instructor at Whitewave, paying him and then hopefully claiming from the Coronavirus Job Retention Scheme at the end of this month…

Runrig aim to stream their final concert next Saturday, I

hope so, and we can all sing along to the final song they ever performed, 'Hearts of Olden Glory' a song of hope, and for a moment, we can be at a festival, in a field with our friends.

I caught a fleeting glimpse
Of life
And though the water's
Black as night
The colours of Scotland
Leave you young inside
There must be a place
Under the sun
Where hearts of olden glory
Grow young

(C & R Macdonald – Runrig)

Friday 17th April

We must celebrate the life we have

Thirty years ago, last weekend we took delivery of our first equipment to set up Whitewave. I only remember the date because it was also Anne's birthday and she was less than impressed at getting ten kayaks and a trailer as a present with sundry paddles and buoyancy aids to go with them. We had a little Renault 5 and each morning during that first season, Anne would drop the kayaks at the old slip in Uig Bay. I would wait by the phone and if I got a booking would bicycle down and meet the clients on the shore.

Had it been less windy, to mark this anniversary we might have taken a couple of kayaks for a paddle at Camus Mor for our appointed daily exercise, but as yet we haven't been out this year, and most of the boats are still in winter storage. Perhaps the next calm day will see us exploring Uamh an Oir, the Cave of Gold, at Bornaskitaig and seeking a glimpse of the monster reputedly residing at the end, presumably surrounded by skeletons of dead pipers if the legend and stories are to be believed.

Looking back, there is relief in our household that the pandemic has hit this year and not the previous, as last year,

I was gaining first-hand experience of home care workers while helping look after my very old father.

He was living in his own house, and eventually and reluctantly allowed carers in twice a day to help get him up and put him to bed. Like many old folks he had the inevitable fall (when found by the care worker he claimed he was 'just checking the skirting boards'). He had a spell in hospital and despite the amazing care he received from the nurses and staff I could see that even pre-corona crisis they were run off their feet. There seemed to be a mélee of controlled chaos, one poor gentleman with Alzheimer's who continually asked for the bill so he could check-out (I bought him a paper each day which seemed to help). A lady had an alarmed cushion which constantly beeped if she stood up as she did a lot. Bored ambulant patients would wonder around looking confused, and there was the inevitable television in the day room with a semi-circle of semi-conscious folk not really watching. Daytime television is a sentence I wouldn't wish on anyone. Amidst all this the staff dispensed drugs and care, food and support.

I am trying to imagine the same scene with the addition of masks, visors and gowns, hiding the smiles of the dedicated staff, and how the necessary virus barriers must also create an obstacle to the emotional support which patients need, and daytime television does not fulfil. One can only hope that Zoom and Facetime is helping create a version of family visit, although I wonder if the older confused mind of a dementia patient can relate to a person on a screen.

With the promise of an increased care package, we managed to get Dad discharged and back to his home, and within the family we provided back up to the care workers, as they would often need extra hands to help move Dad about. Socially distancing would be impossible while helping an old person out of bed. I also learned to change bags, use slip sheets and help feed and even shave him.

We arranged for him to have a DNACPR – This is a document requested by Dad which informs medical professionals 'Do not attempt cardiopulmonary resuscitation'. Common sense really in many situations, but there are medical and societal protocols which, I might suggest, include longevity in life rather than quality.

During this crisis death has taken on a strange statistical bent. Each day we are given numbers of those that have succumbed to Covid 19, league tables are formed and we compare figures between countries while the media discusses NHS areas and the accuracy of the figures and whether they are a correct record. It is as if reducing us to numbers helps distance us from the reality of the fact that people are dying.

Each of these numbers is a father, a mother, a sister, a brother, son or daughter. A person. They have loved and have been loved. They are a relation. Each number was a breathing soul, cared for to the end in difficult circumstances, through mask and visor and more than often without family. If the vulnerable are in isolation, I assume that when they die, they are in isolation and any hand holding near the end is through latex gloves.

It was a privilege to care for my father, but also meet the carers who came in each day, the joy they brought to him as they became part of an extended family. We would always drink coffee and have craic round his bed before attending to any specific need. Dad would always spark up when they visited, and there would often be witty comments, smiles and jokes. They did not know, but they were supporting me as much as Dad.

I imagine that had Dad been alive during this pandemic I would have had to move in with him, rather than driving back and forth, we would have socially isolated, and his neighbours wouldn't have visited to enjoy his wisdom and wit. Maybe the carers wouldn't have been able to drink tea and eat cake with me around his bed as they would be masked up and extra careful around us.

I always think of my Dad when I walk the hills, it was he who first took me up mountains, nurturing my love of the outdoors, fundamental to the development of Whitewave and much of what we have done here in Kilmuir over these past 30 years. When we exercise during this lockdown, whether a kayak, or a cycle or just a saunter along the road, especially in the warmer spring weather, we must celebrate the life we have, and embrace our ability to enjoy it.

Saturday 25th April

As the air clears, we can re-evaluate what is essential in our lives

A few years ago on a beautiful clear morning, we were walking to the monastery on Eilean Chaluim Chille in the drained loch in front of Whitewave in Kilmuir. High up a plane flew over leaving a thick white vapour trail, soon to be followed by another and another. I started counting them and by the time we reached the island, over 30 planes had flown across, each leaving a mark in the sky. The clear blue became hazy, and the afternoon never returned to the clarity of when we began our walk.

These days in lockdown, as we experience this incredible weather, we have the clarity which was lost that day. With few or no airliners flying over, the atmosphere seems sharper, brighter, and maybe pollution from industrial parts usually spreads worldwide, and in the past found its way over to us via jet streams and high air currents. This pollution seems now much reduced.

The talk now is of exit strategies and how we end this lockdown. The term 'other side' has been coined and was even used in last week's very moving front page editorial. What will the other side look like?

There will be many in tough situations during lock down, and for many more the future will be uncertain, and much of the stress from that uncertainty will probably revolve around financial security. A new normal will have to emerge, and we might hope that it will be more sustainable, on all fronts, both locally and globally.

Some say that it was Steve Jobs of Apple computers who turned wants into needs, and empires have been built in our commercial world by making desires into needs. There seem to be business models which require constant expansion or 'biggering', to use a phrase from the well-known Dr Suess' children's book 'The Lorax', which is warning of the consequence of continual industrial growth.

It is always worth looking at nature, even when thinking of economy and industry. Diversity is healthy in the natural world, a healthy ecosystem has an element of sustainability, but within that system, things grow and die, and more importantly are eaten, nothing is wasted. Businesses will come and go, but the reliance on a single sector for a whole community could never be healthy. The tourists are unlikely to visit Skye in the numbers they have in the last few years, and perhaps never will again. There will be no 'go' button pressed after lock-down, and even next season is likely to be considerably quieter. We will have to learn to exist with the reduced numbers. There is risk in business, such is the way of it, I suspect there was a perception that investing in tourism on Skye was a fairly reliable bet. Investing to meet the seemingly never-ending demand was something even banks might have been comfortable with. Looking back at the tourist season last year, maybe it just could not have continued growing and growing. Something had to give, it is just that nobody could have envisaged such a collapse, and for such a reason.

Many of us are guilty of chasing the dollar, but is it for the dollar's sake, is it for needs or wants, and what do we lose in the quest? I used to joke about retiring to the city 'where the pace of life is slower' The cliché of getting a work/life balance sorted is never more relevant.

On my few travels into Portree, I have seen parents playing football with their children in their gardens. I have seen family groups taking their daily exercise, one group having a picnic on a small cnoc above the road, being together, enjoying time together. I have seen on social media, electricians proudly showing off their first loaf of bread, and a joiner with his first batch of home brew bottled. Is this reluctantly filling in time before we go back to normal, or is it learning new behaviours, new ways of being?

Of course, we need the security of paying the mortgage, feeding our families, paying bills, but what are our real needs, and what have we been coerced into thinking we need. During this lockdown, whilst we might have no income, many of us have been gifted that incredibly precious commodity... time.

As the air gets clearer, I would hope that as individuals, communities and a wider society, we can take this opportunity to re-evaluate what is essential, what it is we need. We should look at our lives with the polished unpolluted lens of this lockdown period at what our values and real requirements are and decide what should be on the other side.

I have sat on those planes that fly over, but the stars last night were simply stunning after the evening light had turned from orange to deep, deep blue.

I think we need clarity on the other side.

Chapter Two

May to June 2020

As volunteers we can feel we are doing our bit / From the Blitz to the virus, reducing risk to save lives / In a cash rich time poor society it is maybe community that suffers / Roadside funerals and the confusing areas between obvious extremes / When schools reopen we should remember that education is not all about the classroom / Racism and respect: we should embrace the difference when visitors return to the Highlands / Highland tourism: Like the birds , hoping for an income, fat and seed to feed us after an extra-long winter / We need artists to inspire, entertain and challenge our way of thinking / Timely Salisbury series showed ordinary people doing their best in an unprecedented situation

Saturday 2nd May

As a volunteer we can all feel we are doing our bit

Two or three times a week I have been going into Portree on a motorcycle, and picking up bags of prescriptions from Sandy Grey who collects them from the chemists. I deliver a batch to the hub, an empty holiday cottage in Digg, and these are then distributed to their final destination by a rota of other volunteers. I continue round the North end and deliver those needed in Kilmuir.

During the amazing weather, helping this community service, organised by Myra Macleod through the Skye Community Response Group, has been no hardship. An excuse to ride a fine 800cc Ducati through our incredible landscape on practically empty roads is a total pleasure, and feeling useful to boot is a win-win situation. I was even given fresh bantam eggs by one gentleman.

At Whitewave and home I have continued being busy tidying sheds, painting and finishing an outdoor gravel space I started 15 years ago, but with no likelihood of visitors coming to our place anytime soon, there is something slightly morose and sad about making the buildings and cabins look neat, well maintained and tidy. It all seems a bit soulless and Marie Celeste like with no guests.

Whilst being locked down at home, being busy, fixing and decorating, and even dare I say it, having a good time with family, there is an emerging sense of frustration, even perhaps inadequacy. Others are out there being essential, being key workers and worthwhile, 'fighting' the virus, supporting the vulnerable, while I... make a patio...

I think for many people, there is a need to feel useful, and it is perhaps why for me the motorbike ride is so important. Whilst there is nothing heroic about delivering a few medicines, it gets me out of the house – we might have a big cabin, but it still induces a fever. Being part of a support network and involved in helping the community, works both ways and fulfils a very real need in those helping.

Perhaps everybody wants to feel essential. We can laud the NHS staff, care workers, shop assistants, delivery drivers, but no one is going to clap for the furloughed hospitality workers and idle outdoor instructors, as a volunteer however, we can all feel that we are doing our bit.

There is a huge grey area surrounding the concept of key worker and essential. At first glance, it may seem obvious as to who is key, doctors, nurses, carers and the like but then there are the people who support them. Key workers need paid, so require office staff, they need fed, so also use food shops, they need to get to work, so are likely to drive a vehicle, so they need fuel, and if the car breaks down, they will need a mechanic. They need water and electricity and the internet, and might also need a treat delivered from a mail order company during their well-deserved down time.

Then there are the people who support the people who support the people who support... and so on.

And so there emerges a whole network of service providers, businesses large and small – a web of commerce and production. In order to provide for the frontline, a whole system of interrelated businesses exists, many which might not appear to be essential, but may provide a key element, a small cog in the big picture. In the short term, key workers can perhaps get by, but society shouldn't allow its critical people to just muddle through, as the lockdown period extends, then the need for this support becomes more evident and relevant, and so the web of essentiality widens.

As more roles, jobs and links in society are realised and considered necessary, and indispensability spreads, recreation and tourism, doesn't get much of a look in. We could argue that people need to visit the Old Man of Storr for our economic well-being as much as for their own health and well-being, but for the time being the beds and hot spots will remain empty. So, in order to be relevant and useful, we should perhaps look to our other skills. If tourism is our only income then we have to be creative, not only to make provision but to keep spirit and self-actualisation alive. Economically, if tourism is a second income, the icing on the salaried or pensioned cake, then perhaps we just take the hit, and revert back to a less affluent lifestyle. Many tourist providers left skills and talents in a previous life, perhaps now is the time to revisit and reimagine those skills.

As I understand it, Skye is still waiting. Perhaps by the time this column is online, the virus will be more evident, during this waiting game now more than ever we need to be physically distant, and careful with how we operate. But it is crucial that we also need to look after our mental health and well-being, and so delivering the prescriptions is really as important to volunteer as it is for the receiver. Humans are a social animal, and we need to be part of a community, because we are all essential.

Saturday 9th May

From the Blitz to the virus, reducing risk helps save lives

My father used to tell a story of helping his Dad put out incendiary bombs during the war. Some had landed in their street, and one had set fire to the old lady's garden next door. It was crucial for them to be extinguished, not so much for the fire they caused, but because they were markers for the deadlier high explosive bombs which would follow if they remained lit. Dad used a stirrup pump to spray water over the flames, and the night their street was hit, they were successful in putting out the fires within minutes, returning the area to a blackout, and so escaping the horror of the main bombing run.

Dad also told us of watching the whole sky light up when the town of Coventry, 25 miles away, was hit. The German air force later coined a phrase which translated as 'Coventrified'. It meant completely destroyed.

As a child, my mother lived a few streets from Dad, in a brick terraced house with an outside toilet and back yard. She told of her Dad, keeping pigs in the yard to supplement the wartime rations. When he butchered one, they would eat well, swapping produce as well as helping feed less fortunate neighbours. When I was young we would visit, still in the same house, and I would explore their damp cellar which was full of junk, but I was always excited by the big flag they had down against the wall. It was left over from VE day, 75 years ago, this weekend.

The word 'frontline' has become common parlance as the 'war' against the epidemic is waged. I have never been comfortable with this militaristic language, we can't and don't fight a virus, we just deal with it when it arrives. We will survive it, and when a vaccine is found, or created, we hopefully will be able control the effect and consequence it has on people.

But as the Army arrives on Skye to operate a testing station, perhaps the battle terminology is more appropriate and relevant, and as we anxiously await development, and the further losses which will inevitably happen, we must realise that the war is now on our doorstep, no longer is it just happening elsewhere.

The front as such has arrived on Skye, there have been deaths, and all our thoughts must be with those families and carers most closely affected. My daughter told me of the first death at the care home just as I was about to leave on the prescription run on my motorbike. By Earlish I was in tears, tears for the likelihood that this is probably just the beginning, tears of anger at the state we allowed our NHS to get into, and the fact that care home staff were the bottom of the pile until recently, and still so poorly paid, tears at the fact that still, even now, some people are not following guidelines.

I cannot begin to imagine the emotional toll on the care

staff who must watch this tragedy unfold and play their part with professionalism and dignity, whilst being human, and my heart goes out to those with loved ones still resident in the home.

I don't know anything about warfare, but have heard of Sun Tzu, an ancient Chinese general and philosopher, who wrote 'The Art of War', in it is a famous line which is often only partially quoted as 'know the enemy'.

The lay person might not fully understand the science of virology and how and why viruses mutate, replicate, take over the cells in our bodies, attack our tissues and cause infection, but by now, most people have a general awareness of what needs to be done to help slow or prevent the spread. We know our enemy well enough.

Sun Tzu's quote is actually 'If you know your enemy and yourself then you need not fear the outcome of battle'. His crucial advice is to know ourselves during warfare.

Perhaps we should take this opportunity to get to know ourselves, consider our actions and behaviours, and do what we need to do in order to help slow the spread and minimise the tragedy. There are other vulnerable people on Skye, not just in care homes. Our friends, relatives and neighbours, many of them are vulnerable. Now more than ever we need to follow social distancing, wear masks if we are in shops or likely to be near other people. It is all about reducing risk, a bit like my Dad putting out the bomb markers or sticking up blackout paper on the windows all those years ago, doing what they could to save lives, possibly their own.

Considering how many bombs were dropped on Coventry, remarkably few people were killed. They were ready, many in shelters and many having trekked to safety outside the city, to watch from afar their homes being destroyed.

We perhaps could have been more prepared, but hindsight is a wonderful thing. When it is all over, we can argue and examine the protocols and recommendations, and perhaps hold some decision makers to account, but for now the important thing is to prevent further deaths and help those helping us. It is all down to our actions and choice, and our level of integrity.

My thoughts and sympathies are with all the people who have been affected by the recent deaths.

Saturday 16th May

In a cash rich, time poor society, it is maybe community that suffers

I was brought up in a small village in Lancashire but closely bordering both Yorkshire and Cumbria. It had a church with a tower, a primary school, three farms and a pub, but no shop. It wasn't quite the quintessential English village as there was no green, but plenty of woods, a river and streams, and fields and lanes for a boy to run feral. We lived in the first new development, nine houses built in what would have been the grounds of the 'big house', now the pub.

Not much has changed to look at in the village since unusually there has been no more house building except all the barns we used to play in are now fancy homes, and I have no idea where the bales of hay are stored. I guess they are now big bales of silage wrapped in plastic piled up on the edges of the fields until needed.

One day when walking with my best pal to primary school (I am not sure if the children do that now) we named every inhabitant in every house in the village. There were probably sixty or seventy houses all told, and we knew everybody.

I am not sure if anyone living in the village could do that now, let alone two ten-year-old boys.

It was the same on Skye, when my wife Anne was wee, she knew everybody in Kilmuir. On going up to High School and through choirs, drama. cèilidhs and community events she then got to know of a fair proportion of those from the wider community.

Last year she was at a cèilidh in the hall, 'How are you enjoying your holiday?' she asked two strangers '...erm we live here.' they replied.

Communities have changed.

We can all make a stab at the reasons, from kids being less feral, and not getting to know their old neighbours, everybody being more frightened, enveloping children with cotton wool and many being timetabled to within a second of bedtime, both parents working often in the nearest bigger place, people generally spending less time in the locales they live in, many often only returning home to sleep. As our way of earning money has developed, perhaps our need for the neighbour changes. We don't borrow, we buy, and we don't need help with the hay, we don't need a cup of sugar.

Emails, computer games, Netflix and Facebook, as well as more traditional screen fare, all vie for attention, but as technology sucks away our time it also fills the void of a local disconnection, it is perhaps not all detrimental, it is about connectivity.

My son could no way name all the people living in Kilmuir, but when he was 14 we visited my Dad and my 'home' village. Within an hour of arriving, through snapchat, messenger and maybe even a traditional text message, he had contacted friends he knew from bike racing who lived in the north of England, and arranged a ride. It did necessitate an hour's drive to a pickup /drop off at a motorway service station (I think he ended up riding in Wales but that is another story) His virtual community became real for the day.

Our spread of family across country and continent can seem a little closer through video conversations, and now is much easier than the old annual and often tearful Christmas Day phone conversation to relatives in Australia.

But as our community spreads geographically, what is in danger of being lost are the rooted local links, the cèilidh round the kitchen table is perhaps being replaced with a Zoom conversation to New South Wales. During these eight weeks of lockdown for many the screen has been a saving grace, allowing vital contact with friends and family, but perhaps more importantly, the pandemic has also instigated a reimagining of physical local community, with the huge growth of support networks and people wanting to help.

Skye Community Response has been exemplary, logistical precision with military style efficiency, linking into more local organisations. Prescriptions delivered, food vouchers given out, cooked meals provided, messages picked up, money raised. But also enabling conversations. The Ducati is great for that, (who wouldn't want to discuss their medicines being delivered on such fine Italian engineering). When I deliver prescriptions, most people want a chat.

And it is 'community' who may know who is in need, and more crucially the subtle ways of facilitating that help. People are proud and we have lost the way of asking for help. There may be a fine line between nosiness and general interest, but it is often our neighbours who will know if we are struggling. Nosiness in community is often borne out of concern and compassion. The old vulnerable gentleman living alone might need some help, but so too that young family whose wage earner missed out on furlough or self-employment grants, or the single person who would normally be working in a hotel, but hasn't had an income for months. It might not be obvious.

On my last prescription run, one lady asked me 'Is this service just for the crisis?' I was suitably vague in my reply, as we don't know how long measures will be in place, and as yet how it will all end, but perhaps community has been reawakened. As we move to 'the other side' perhaps we should be mindful of the benefits to the community of community. We should keep a balance of global and local, virtual and physical, and make sure they complement each other symbiotically. We are likely to continue Zoom meetings with distant friend and relatives, why shouldn't we continue delivering prescriptions.

The irony is that organised committees are creating the infrastructures that used to exist organically in the past. Buses used to deliver papers and prescriptions, although you might have only got your paper once the person picking it up for you had read it. If you were sick, food would appear. A lot of community never went away, but perhaps became less evident and more fragile as we all became busier and more money and work driven. In a cash rich, time poor society, it is maybe community that suffers.

We might not need help with the hay, or a cup of sugar, but we do need our local community. I may challenge P7 children to learn who all their neighbours are, and on the other side, maybe at the next cèilidh, we will know everyone in the hall.

Our community has lost Ina Beaton, possibly its oldest inhabitant. My condolences go to her famiy – *Mairidh gaol is ceol.*

Saturday 23rd May

Roadside funerals and the confusing areas between obvious extremes

I attended my first 'drive by' funeral last Saturday. Betty Campbell used to run the Ferry Inn in Uig when I first came to Skye. You didn't see her very often, but they say she knew exactly what was going on in her bar, which could be lively and inertia inducing. When Anne and I were young and fun to be with, we could lose a whole weekend after only intending a quick one on a Friday night... Betty also did the school dinners, and one of my friends commented that as a child, he remembered her dressing well even in the canteen, and how she was always very glamorous when 'dishing up the Angel Delight'.

We parked the Ducati opposite the old Police Station in Uig and waited with others for the hearse to roll by. The funeral director acknowledged our nods and bowed heads with a knowing look and slow wave. It was all very appropriate and as poignant as it was short.

Ina Beaton's drive by was at Kilmalaug, and we stood in a passing place on the road to the graveyard. I heard that the family found it very moving to see so many people stood in drives, gateways and road ends showing their respects...

By the time this piece is online, we will have been to Charlie Mackinnon's. I remember 10 years ago, giving him and my father-in-law Calum Martin, their pensions on the last day we ran the Linicro Post Office at Whitewave...

On a happier note, last weekend was my enforced run in aid of Skye Camanachd's amazing Land's End to John O Groats challenge for the Skye Response Group. We duly downloaded the Strava App which magically and frustratingly enables a phone to log physical effort, reducing sweat and toil to a red line on a map and some statistics that only athletes and enthusiasts understand.

As I detest running, I may have suggested that my son take all our phones in his pocket on his mountain bike but was told in no uncertain terms that this would be cheating, and not entering into the spirit of a challenge.

Rubha Huinis is one of my favourite places in the world, so we used the challenge as an excuse to drive the short distance and make the run a change from our daily walk through the common grazing.

If I have been there once, I have been there a hundred times with school groups. youth groups, corporate adults and tourists. It never fails to inspire.

As well as its incredible outlook, it is a fabulous place for spotting cetaceans, which can often be seen from the cliff tops, although the most spectacular experience I had was while kayaking round the point. On this occasion, a minke whale surfaced several times a few feet to our right, as a pod of tiny porpoises were rising to our left. Each huge, long leviathanic exhalation would be interspersed with a series of short staccato breaths from the porpoises...

One visit, during winter, walking with a mixed corporate and young person's group from Columba 1400, saw us arrive at the Coastguard's lookout as the sun was beginning to set way to the southwest, while at the same time and same height, a full moon was rising way over to the northeast. As the sun sank, the moon rose, as if they were in balance and Rubha Huinis was the fulcrum of a massive celestial seesaw, and the centre of our universe.

When I am at the clifftop with a group, I am always a little nervous. It is indeed a three-hundred-foot drop which would be a very sudden death if you fell off. When I warn people, I will often however use humour, I suggest that whilst the fall would kill them, I would be subsequently buried with paperwork, or that if they fell off it would spoil my favourite place for me, as I would have difficulty revisiting it without remembering their tragic demise...

In truth, I have to use judgement, if a group is lively and boisterous then I may be very authoritarian – 'DO NOT GO PAST THIS POINT' and on occasion, I won't take a group there. American students can be the worst, 'Don't worry John, I go hiking in Colorado' as one insists on standing just a bit too close for my comfort.

Then there was the group from the inner-city homeless charity, one of whom looked at me and asked, 'Does it ever make you want to jump?'

My job when leading a group in the outdoors includes a continual and dynamic risk management, most of which is not so much the outdoor environment, but really people's response to it. Weather forecasts, decisions about routes, navigation and technical knowledge are all quite easy, what is crucial is the judging of a group that you don't know and working out how they will cope, and how they may react to the environment and activity.

There is a thing called perceived risk which is different to real risk and comes about through a lack of understanding or knowledge. Often people think things are dangerous when they are not. Conversely, complacency and familiarity can mask real risk, and people will court dangers knowingly, but unwittingly. I was given the example of fiddling with a mobile phone while driving. Because it is familiar, we forget how dangerous it is.

Risk assessments are based on an easy formula. How likely is it to happen, and what is the outcome? If it is really probable, and the outcome is death, then don't do it, if it is really unlikely and the consequence is, well inconsequential, then on you go... Of course life, adventure activity and viral infection all exists in the grey confusing area in between the obvious extremes.

As a route map to easing lockdown is announced, we have to play our part in reducing risk, but importantly we have to take responsibility in managing risk, to ourselves, and more importantly to others. The risk might be minimal of spreading Covid in the Co-Op, but if the consequence to the person behind us in the queue is significant, because they are vulnerable, then we should help minimise the risk, by wearing a mask, and if the person in front of us is young and healthy, remember, they might have a vulnerable parent at home. We have to act as if we are all vulnerable. The decisions we make in this lockdown transition will have to be mindful of others and the bigger picture.

Saturday 23rd May 2020 • 57

Nicola Sturgeon said the route map is 'not written in stone'. It's correct to be flexible and dynamic as if society is like one of my groups walking to Rubha Huinis – behaviour and responsibility will dictate whether we can enjoy a picnic on the clifftop, or if the risk of falling off will still be too great.

Saturday 30th May

When schools reopen, we should remember that education is not all about the classroom

'NoWrongPath' is a social media movement, which aims to provide inspiration and reassurance to young people receiving their exam results. It illustrates that there are many varied routes and paths in life, and that ways are often not straight, traditional or obvious, a theme being to get people to recount their journeys in life, often concentrating on those who did less well academically.

I left school with a few 'O' Levels and two mediocre 'A' Levels, D's I think, barely passes. I had discovered motorbikes, girls, and rock and roll – probably in response and rebellion to having been dragged up every mountain by my parents as soon as I could walk. For a number of years, I would do anything but climb mountains. When I was 22, I rode my motorbike to and through the Middle East.

A few years later, my country dropped bombs on a town in Serbia, the former Yugoslavia, where I had drunk beers and partied with folk, and In Syria I was taken in by families who might now be in refugee camps – or more likely dead.

Riding through the Golan Heights where ten years

previously the Yom Kippur war had raged, there were still abandoned villages with bullet-ridden walls. I drank tea with Arabs, and I picked bananas and aubergines with Israelis.

It is probably safe to assume that these experiences had as great an influence on my outlook on life as any lesson, lecture or exam.

Academically, although I loved reading and writing, my school wouldn't let me take English 'A' level as I had failed the 'O' level, despite this a few years later I obtained an English degree, and I seem to be able to string a sentence together for this column...

I have run an outdoor centre for 30 years, and whilst never making it as a musician (we made a record but nobody bought it!) my love of music and the arts has remained and hopefully has helped Anne in her professional career. I still occasionally pick up the bass, and I can scratch a half decent tune out on the fiddle. At school I never got beyond 'Three Blind Mice' on the recorder.

When my kids were 5 and 11, we took them round the world for 6 months, visiting India, Australia, Fiji and America – my mantra being Mark Twain's quote 'Never let schooling get in the way of a good education.'

Things have suddenly got very different. In the past weeks and months children have been schooled at home via the Internet. Teachers have transferred the blackboard to the screen, and the kitchen table has become the classroom. Whilst before some pupils emailed their homework in, now it is all emailed, all homework.

Of course this has presented challenges, frustrations and inequalities, just like traditional schooling. Some young people engage well, others not, some teachers engage well, others not. Just like traditional schooling.

The talk and plan is that schools will reopen physically after summer, possibly and probably in a very different manner. It seems however that there is a rush to adapt an old norm to a new unknown reality. This is understandable, as change is always uncertain, and it is safe to stick with what you know, but perhaps we will be missing an opportunity to create a new reality. Begin afresh with a blank piece of paper.

If our best creative thinkers were asked to make a framework for educating young people, starting with a blank sheet of paper, with today's technologies would they build the institutions we have today? Would they build a school?

Perhaps this is unfair on the classes of 2020 or 2021 and further, experimenting with them and their futures, so we will undoubtedly keep things as normal as possible, but flux seems to have been the norm, with curriculum change and continual development. There have been plenty experiments in the past. It is already quite radical to have suggested staggered start times, blended learning and a concentration on screen contact. Perhaps national exam level provision could develop into a drop-in style of tutorial seminar-based provision, where a school is a resource to be used as required, and not attended per se. Perhaps the new normal could have place-centred outdoor learning as its core.

I heard one teacher complain on the radio, 'We are educationalists, not child minders'. There seems to be a blurring between parenting, social work and education, and schools appear to being used as a solution to all society's ills, becoming all things to all people.

The role that schools have played over and above teaching has become evident during Covid and lockdown as parents have had to look after their children continuously. Situations are all unique, and there will have been a whole spectrum from embraced appropriate enjoyable home learning, to dysfunctional chaos. Most families have probably been somewhere in the middle, but sadly schools in some cases have had to continue providing a haven for vulnerable children.

Most importantly there is 'NoWrongPath' even more so today when destinations may be more uncertain. Resilience, empathy, creativity and integrity will be what our children need in the future.

I think the class of 2020 will be fine, they have had a unique experience which will help make them who they become. Travel is likely to be harder in the near future, how easy it will it be to take a family around the world or ride a motorbike a long distance for a gap year might be debatable, but there will always be opportunity for experiential adventure. Routes back into traditional education are always available, perhaps even more so now. I suspect universities will be desperate for students, so will be creating access courses to enable those with uncertain schooling certificates.

When I was caught 'skiving' PE (I hated PE) I had no idea I would end up running an outdoor activity centre. When I was failing Physics 'A' Level at school, I had no idea I would end up with a Master's degree from Edinburgh University. Whilst the First Law of Thermodynamics (energy cannot be created or destroyed and the total quantity of energy in the universe stays the same) is a crucial and fabulous bit of knowledge, it probably isn't what helped me when my motorbike gearbox stuck in Jericho.

Saturday 5th June

Racism and respect: we should embrace the different cultures when visitors return to the Highlands

Last Tuesday many people blacked out their profile pictures on social media in solidarity with the 'BlackLivesMatter' campaign and in outrage at the killing of George Floyd in Minneapolis. A police officer had held him down with his knee on his neck for over 8 minutes.

Black Lives Matter as an organisation wasn't created in response to this incident but has been around for seven years, originating after the killing of a black teenager in Florida.

Discussing racism is often difficult. It is easy to black out our pictures, write suitably appropriate sentences showing our abhorrence at brutality, and adding liberal and rational support to communities on the other side of the world. But actually discussing, trying to understand and reason why is difficult, because it questions humanity, culture and even our own place and identity.

One of my friends was complaining, understandably, about nearly being knocked off his bicycle by two cars. He added that they were 'full of Asians' driving erratically. His point was actually the slipping of lockdown and the onset of visitors, and not I believe the race of those visitors, but their colour was an identifying feature, and he made comment. We often find ourselves using race and colour in this way. Similarly, I might mention Asians who stayed in our wigwam cabins, but if it is related to something negative I confess to sometimes feeling uncomfortable if I find myself mentioning race as I speak. I occasionally wonder if I am sounding racist, or whether I am just being too sensitive to some politically correct protocol.

People look different, and much of it is accidental and geographical. If you were born in Baghdad or Delhi, you would probably have browner skin than if you were born in Uig, and possibly a lighter skin colour than should you have been born in Nairobi. It is all an accident of birth and is to do with the amount of melanin in the body, which protects against harmful ultra-violet sunlight.

The culture people are born into is also accidental, again if you were born in Baghdad, then you are likely to be Arabic and Islamic, if born in Delhi then you might be Hindi or Sikh. Kenyans are more likely to be Christian. In Scotland, your type of Christianity might also depend on location; Catholics and protestants coming from fairly well-defined geographical areas. Of course, culture is more than religion, but even for non-adherents and atheists, it is often a significant part of the richness of the societies we live in.

I was in Bali, Indonesia earlier this year during the festival of Galungan. The place was literally dripping with decorations. Ornate and huge 'penjor' lined the roads and adorned buildings, taller than telegraph poles and more prevalent, they were beautifully twisted and plaited from palm fronds. Shrines and offerings were everywhere, it was vibrant, colourful and beautiful. It was a religious festival, but totally embedded in the culture of the Balinese, in the way Christmas is in Scotland.

Balinese people are amongst the friendliest I have come across in all my travels, a genuine warmth in their demeanour. Balinese folk are brown in colour, because it is very sunny in Indonesia; they have evolved to have more melanin, and therefore more protection against the sun.

We don't choose the colour of our skin, or the culture we are born into, but what we do with our lot is a product of our upbringing, our wider society experience and everything that has happened to us. Most of our behaviour is due to nurture not nature and is down to choice. Our values and empathies lie in our reaction to our experience and learning from consequence. The problem stems in that much of that experience lies out with our control.

If we are black, poor and have been persecuted by institutional society since birth, we might take to the streets. When pepper sprayed or met with water cannon, rubber bullet or tear gas, we might resort to throwing rocks, petrol bombs. Windows might be broken, we might loot.

If our role model father figure is a gun toting white supremacist, we might believe ourselves to have a greater entitlement than those of a different colour.

We would be wrong.

These are extreme examples. Rationalising and trying to understand the actions of others is fraught with generalisation and perhaps cliché. We can never know what makes a person act the way they do, and we can only imagine being in their shoes, and seeing through the lens of their eyes.

What is as tragic as a police officer killing another human being in a slow seemingly deliberate fashion, is that a society, its culture and institutions can produce someone capable and accepting of such an action. I hope the killer will be brought to justice, and that a grieving family can find peace and forgiveness, but more importantly, can we heal the society that produces this behaviour?

Most of the ills are due to poverty, deprivation, and the inequality of opportunity.

Fear and ignorance is layered on top, with greed and entitlement. Power normally resides with the rich, who want to stay rich.

The cry is that we are all the same underneath, black, white, brown or yellow, and yet we are all different, unique products of vastly different culture, geography, upbringing, beliefs and experience. We are both the same and both different, and this confusing contradiction should be embraced, celebrated and above all respected.

Scotland is known for celebrating diversity, but it is more than the music, the festivals, the ceremonies and the food, it is the people and their attitudes and their experience we should celebrate.

It may be sometime before visitors from other continents arrive back to the Highlands in any number, but our communities as hosts are in a perfect situation to embrace the cultures brought and above all respect both differences and similarities.

Saturday 13th June

Highland tourism: Like the birds, hoping for an income, fat and seed to feed us after an extra-long winter

We have a bird feeder hanging in the tree outside my kitchen window. It can suck away quite a lot of my time, as I watch the antics of the birds it attracts, reed buntings with their wonderful Edwardian moustache markings, ubiquitous sparrows, goldfinch which almost seem too colourful to be allowed here, beautiful gold flashes on the wings, with bright red faces, shouldn't they be living in some tropical clime. They look made up ready to perform some contemporary dance act, or seventies glam rock show.

And then there are the starlings. I think they are my favourite, equally as colourful as the goldfinch, with an iridescent shine in the sun. They also mimic sounds from their surroundings and can sound like phones and car alarms embedded in their complex song patterns.

There has been a lot of bickering of late around the feeder, adult starlings feeding their fairly grown-up kids that look old enough to fend for themselves. The slightly duller browner juveniles scream and jostling on the branch next to the food supply; 'me first me first' as the parent removes a seed from the dangling cage and thrusts it down the throat of its boisterous offspring, in a veritable feeding frenzy. Like lockdown meals with children?

If the feeder runs out of fat seed balls, the birds disappear, to find either a natural food supply, or another human patron.

As July the 15th has been marked on year planners and in diaries, and a possible restart to aspects of the tourist industry looms, I am not sure if the birds are like the visitors descending on our communities, briefly eating and flying away, or if we the providers are the birds, desperately hoping for an income, fat and seed to feed us after an extra-long winter.

Social media fluttered with posts from businesses stating, 'We hope to be open', the sensible ones being aware of Fergus Ewing's proviso, 'This date cannot be definitive and is conditional on public health advice and progression to phase three of the route map. '

Whilst a lot of work will need to be done, practicalities and protocols worked out, how do we clean rooms, how do we 'meet and greet', do we leave rooms fallow for 72 hours, do we use PPE when cleaning, I think as much work needs to be done in the wider community.

How are the visitors going to eat, how are they going to shop? I have seen some quite lax adherence to protection in local shops with face covering usage fairly minimal at best. We have probably got away with this behaviour due to the low numbers of cases outwith the care home community. This could change with an influx of people from away. Any vigilantism must be directed at ourselves and the messages we put out when we go about our day-to-day business as lockdown eases. Protect ourselves and others.

Those vulnerable people we have been looking after with prescription runs and message collections, some of them might not be looking forward to an influx of staycationers. What else are they bringing with their much-needed cash?

None of these problems are insurmountable. Guidelines will be available and in the month, ahead, confidence will hopefully return and a dose of common sense will go a long way to making things work.

The talk is that furlough is just the precursor to redundancy, and the economy will be struggling in all sectors. The knock-on is likely to be fewer visitors with less money, and of course with the quarantine enforcement for overseas visitors, there won't be many coming from afar.

I hope the tourism return will be a trickle, then a stream, in order for us all to get used to how it can work. Despite being involved in the business I actually hope that it never returns to the flood, the tsunami of the last two years, where the danger was the destruction of our environment and our community. We were perhaps too busy making money to spend time with our families, friends and neighbours.

Whilst loving the quiet roads, the time spent with family, and the time spent revaluating priorities (as well as painting anything that doesn't move and fixing everything that has been broken) it couldn't last for ever. The savings are being eaten into, the government assistance also doesn't last forever, reality looms.

There is an economic model of price and product determination, that everybody is acutely aware of called 'supply and demand'. In recent years as the visitor numbers went through the roof, and perhaps became unsustainable, bed provision rose, spare rooms developed, cabins and pods built, garages renovated. Still numbers rose, and so did the prices, a simple correlation.

There is likely to now be an oversupply of bed provision, the economists would foresee a reduction in price as people compete for a smaller market. This may at first bring prices down to a realistic level, there was perhaps a danger that Skye was becoming a rich person's destination. A possible consequence may be what I have heard described as, 'A race to the bottom', with what is effectively a price war, and possibly falling too far. This when the product suddenly has become more expensive to manage, rooms costing more to clean, hotels only being able to cope with fewer guests to comply with social distancing.

We have a free market economy, there is little or no control, people can charge what they like, and undercutting is a valid entrepreneurial technique; do something better cheaper...!

I mentioned weeks ago, for many, the tourist dollar is the icing on the pension cake, a second income to a professional wage. Perhaps there is a fine line between need and greed. Some tourist operators have been forced to use food banks and needing help from the Skye Community Response group during lockdown. As business returns, and these people can begin rebuilding their livelihoods, perhaps others have to decide what their own needs are. The pension or the wage might be enough.

One of the reasons I love starlings are the incredible

murmurations they create in autumn, just before roosting in the evenings. These bickering birds who flutter and jostle around the trees, for twenty minutes or so before descending to reeds and branch to sleep, put on a display with no equal in nature. Moving in unison, they create patterns in the sky, shapes, forms, dance. Apparently, each bird affects the six or seven around it but a flock of tens of thousands moves as if one, producing something beautiful.

Community can be like that.

Saturday 19th June

We need artists to inspire, entertain, and challenge our way of thinking

'Skye's the Limit' is a fund-raising exercise challenge set by Skye Event's, who amongst other things would normally have organised the Skye Half Marathon last weekend. A plan at present is for it hopefully to run on the 31st October. The idea of the current Covid challenge is to walk, run or cycle as many miles as possible as a team throughout the month of June, and raise money for Skye Community Response.

Team White/Martin decided to take the opportunity, stretch the 5-mile exercise travelling guideline a little, and check the trig point out on top of the Storr.

Nearly every time I see the old man, some memory flashes up of that incredible event held 15 years ago 'The Storr Unfolding Landscape' was a night-time adventure, when the arts organisation NVA audaciously lit up the paths wood and hillside, painting the rocks and trees with spotlight and projection. Poetry sounds and song also echoed around Am Bodach, adding to the sometime ethereal experience.

I was in charge of safety, and it is not without some pride I can say we took nearly 6000 folk up the hill, at night, in all weathers over a period of 6 weeks, and at worst had one twisted ankle. Each participant was given a head torch and as if pilgrims, a stout stick. A team of guides dictated the progress of three groups who had to pass at exactly the right point. It was a single track, with few passing places. Radio contact with a coordinating control centre at Storr Lochs monitored the flow, as the audience became part of the show with lines of lights stretching across parts of the hill. There was precision in the art.

And it was art.

At the time the WHFP wrote 'Some people say that any addition to the Storr is at worst sacrilege, at best gilding the lily. Yet, on reflection we can see it's possible to do just that, and do it acceptably... This may be the aesthetics of the future'.

At first, my delight was the facilitation of getting people outside, at night, helping give them an outdoor experience. Any art was a bonus; first and foremost they were having a safe adventure. But as the weeks rolled by I became more and more mesmerised by the art, and took my own understanding of what it may or may not have meant.

It was Orson Welles who wrote, 'I don't know much about art, but I know what I like', but art amongst other things, can and perhaps should make you think.

Now more than ever we need to do a lot of thinking.

Knowing what we like is valid, but the danger is we stay within our comfort zone and remain unchallenged in our thinking.

Art can be pretty, it can be disgusting, it can be clever, it can seemingly be not, it can entertain, it can stimulate.

Some could say the 'Storr Unfolding Landscape' did all of these...

Above all it made me look at a place differently, in the reactions of the participants, as well as the aesthetics of the event itself. I saw people's faces in awe at the display in the corrie, I saw some fed up in the rain.

I could hear a pin drop at Anne Martin's live singing echoing off the cliff from 'her cnoc' as the 50 or so lights, some as far away as Raasay and Ben Tianavaig were programmed to automatically turn on, some nights mirroring the stars in the sky. Occasionally I could barely hear the song through the wind.

As she sang, some nights due to the direction of the wind and the subsequent noise to her microphone, she would have her back to the audience and as a small silhouette in the distance they were unaware that she sang to the landscape and not them. She says it was a privilege to be able to perform in the landscape of the song and yes, she understood the songs differently by the end. She told me that she would sometimes have a feeling of her words floating off across the Sound of Raasay, to drift forever, perhaps to be heard randomly in some far off place. Maybe the answer really is, 'blowing in the wind'.

There is often criticism of big art, especially if public money is spent. Criticism is actually part of the point.

Often the cry is that surely the money could be better spent on roads, health or education, anything useful, but I believe it is a mark of a civilised society, firstly how the old, infirm and poor are treated, but secondly and still importantly how art and culture are patronised.

If society is purely utilitarian, then we might as well give up now. We need our artists, musicians, writers, poets and free thinkers to inspire, entertain, but also to challenge our way of thinking.

Art can make you see things differently, by making statements, either loud or subtle. Artist Jeanne-Claude Denat de Guillebon, who died in November last year, was made famous in 1995 along with Christo Vladimirov Javacheff by wrapping Berlin's Reichstag with material. A bold statement if ever there was one.

I often smile when I see Am Bodach and do take delight in explaining to visitors the Gaelic roots to it's descriptive name and their anatomical connotations. Clothing the huge upstanding stone volcanic intrusion, could, well, some might see it as appropriate, even the decent thing to do!

We see graffiti appearing on some statues, and the toppling of one is a powerful image, ironically reminiscent of the falling of dictatorship. Imagine the power of statues wrapped, covered non-destructively in material. Temporary shrouding to stimulate reasoned debate on their relevance or not in the future. I guess the thugs would rip it off...

As we cycle run or walk to keep fit and challenge our bodies and log our miles for Skye's the Limit, we should also challenge our minds. Look at the familiar as if through an artist's eyes. imagine viewing through the lens of others, visitors. Maybe even plan a return when the nights draw in, which they will soon enough. Shine a torch at a rock, a tree, listen to some song, capture an image, maybe write some poetry.

We are all artists.

Saturday 27th June

Timely Salisbury series showed ordinary people doing their best in an unprecedented situation

I don't own a television and haven't lived in a house with one since leaving the parental home way back last century. My kids seemed to have survived this oversight in their upbringing although in high school it apparently caused some surprise amongst their pals. I should add it is not all books by candlelight, we do have movie nights in winter when we watch DVD's and now Netflix through a data projector onto a large pull-down screen. It is almost a cinematic experience with the sound coming through my old-fashioned stereo and its big speakers on the wall.

Very occasionally though I get to hear about a television drama that sparks an interest. Mostly they are forgotten as if they are any good, they are released on DVD or online as a mini-series, like Sherlock, produced by Skye's own Douglas Mackinnon, and I can enjoy them at my leisure, glass and popcorn in hand whilst lying on a sofa.

Last week however I heard about the BBC drama Salisbury Poisonings, an adaption of the real events following the attempted murder of a former Russian spy in 2018, and the ensuing public health danger. The series was timely, there was talk of tracking and tracing, areas were locked down, and there was a possible spread of an invisible deadly nerve agent.

Containment was the key.

Viewers now have an understanding and comprehension about much of the unfolding events, that they perhaps wouldn't' have had, were it screened four months earlier. Contamination through contact from surfaces such as light switches and work surfaces, and Salisbury business owners complaining at a public meeting of 95% drop in trade due to the cordons in their streets. Much of what happened would strike a chord with many, as would the uncertainty of it all.

I managed to watch the three episodes, albeit a few days after they were broadcast, and was struck how the story was a human one. It was about ordinary people doing the best they could in an unprecedented situation. It was seemingly very true to life, the screenplay being written after many interviews with the real players, who we meet very briefly at the end in a very moving vignette.

The main protagonist was director of public health for the local authority Tracy Daszkiewicz, who finds herself transported from doing the school run on the way to her perhaps ordinary council job, to making decisions in overflowing conference rooms with senior Police officers, Porton Down chemical warfare experts and Whitehall representatives, the outcome of which could either prevent or mitigate the deaths of thousands of people.

At times Daszkiewicz sits in her car with her head on the steering wheel, fighting back the tears and trying not to be overcome by the gravity of it all.

Her agenda quite simply, was to protect the health of the people.

As lockdown begins to be eased in Scotland, we know well enough that there is a balance between lives and livelihoods, health and the economy, mental and physical well-being, and consequence for the future. Decisions are being made daily as to how to ease the country back into a new normality in the most appropriate manner.

These decisions are beginning to be politicised, and the old adversarial ways are beginning to rear their ugly heads in the chambers of our government. It is correct that decisions are scrutinised, and justification is asked for in public, but knee jerk criticism for political posturing is untimely, and often disingenuous. We are still very much in a public health crisis. The future is unknowable, and whatever path is taken, there will be negative consequences. It is not at all cut and dried or in any way unambiguous.

Mark Twain popularised the quote 'lies, damned lies and statistics', but numbers are persuasive. If we are to believe the figures gleaned from the internet, England with 10 times the population has approximately 60 times the average daily new cases and hospital admissions, and 40 times the deaths.

In England, the Westminster government is handling the crisis differently, perhaps with a different agenda and a different emphasis on the balance between the health of the economy and the health of the population. Perhaps they have different priorities, but I have medic friends who are glad they live in Scotland and worry how things might pan out south of the border.

Saturday 27th June 2020

Lockdown couldn't, and cannot last forever, the new normal must include commerce which must include tourism, but when I hear tourism representatives arguing for a reduction in the distance of social distances in order to protect jobs and businesses, I wonder, how many extra deaths should we allow in order to allow a pub to open. There are always different viewpoints and it takes real wisdom to be able to consider all perspectives. When the lobbyists and business sector leaders want relaxations to protect their interests, I hope they realise the bigger picture, and no decision which may preclude their ruin would be taken lightly or flippantly. The collateral damage of closed-down businesses I am sure will weigh heavily on the consciousness of our political leaders.

I am reminded of a cartoon I have seen used in conflict resolution courses, two people are looking at a number drawn on the floor from opposite angles, with the phrase, 'just because you are right doesn't mean to say I am wrong'.

The number is of course a 6. Or is it a 9?

It is clear that the sliding and phasing of the opening of tourism and recreational facilities is to keep a slowly, slowly approach to prevent a flood of movement of people and the virus. They could have said folk with brown eyes are allowed out on Tuesdays and Thursdays, anything to stem a possible tide.

An aspect of leadership is to be able to make difficult decisions, taking all criteria on board often in the face of criticism, trying to see the big picture in the face of uncertainty. A change of decision, a backtrack or U-turn seems to be regarded as weakness by an opposition, although I have never understood why. Surely it shows strength of character to realise that a chosen path might not be the best, and that a different option might be better.

There has been some discussion about female leaders acting differently and perhaps more appropriately in the face of the current pandemic. I wonder if Salisbury was lucky having a female director of health. If the poisoning drama is to be believed, Tracy Daszkiewicz acted with incredible professionalism and complete integrity, with compassion and humanity. Political allegiances aside I believe that the same could be said of our own leader in Holyrood, a person doing an extraordinary job in an unprecedented situation.

I wonder if Nicola Sturgeon sometimes stops her car, puts her head on the steering wheel and weeps at the gravity of it all.

Chapter Three

July to August 2020

We should take time to plant seeds in the ground and in our minds / In search of Skye's lesser known treasures / Attitudes cross borders as easily as migrating birds and viral infections / Litter is a not an urban or rural condition but a human one / Rediscovering the art of face-to-face conversation / Print is not immune from lies but at least there is some accountability / After the exams, will we address the real reasons for inequality / Why do some folk always seem to sit on the angry side of the fence? / Think of the future, and the immortal jellyfish

(7th August the WHFP returns to print)

Saturday 4th July

We should take time to plant seeds in the ground and in our minds

My family thought I had finally lost it when I announced that as a final lockdown project I was going to construct a woodland walk.

Skye is not well known for its trees, and Kilmuir unless you look very carefully, has at best fewer than most.

There are plenty of the ubiquitous willows. We all plant those, just stick a branch in a damp bit of ground and chances are within 4 or 5 years there will be something that may just about count as a tree. They are also pretty good at spreading themselves.

Over 50 years ago, I believe crofters were assisted in developing tiny patches of forestry. There was a scheme which a few took advantage of, planting the other ubiquitous species; pine. They never really looked right, hence those square blocks of the wrong green, often with windfall at the edges, presumably as the roots were not deep enough to withstand our January gales. Some have now been cut down, like the big plantations which are now being harvested, but I don't know if these crofting forests were meant to provide, firewood, shelter beds or perhaps just job creation in their planting.

18 years ago, I planted an area between my house and the road. I say area, more a large postage stamp patch, not even a tennis court, and on a slope at that. I put in indigenous broad-leaved species. Slow growing, but mainly of correct provenance for the north of Skye.

My trees struggled for years, and nobody ever really noticed them, but then one year we realised we couldn't see our wigwam cabins or the wind turbine from the kitchen window, there was foliage in the way. More usefully, people couldn't see us.

My trees had grown up.

Some had managed to attain the dizzy heights of 15 or even 16 feet, and at least one has a bird's nest in its branches.

I probably planted them too close together. When you put a tiny sapling in the ground, it is difficult to imagine it years later as an actual tree, competing for light and resource. Perhaps there is method in allowing a dense growth to provide communal shelter while small, and then sacrifice a percentage to allow others to grow more robustly and efficiently.

Survival of the fittest by management.

My woodland was quite dense, and it was clear that one or two were struggling. If those were taken out, not only would it help the others, but there would be space to walk through. I could enjoy my trees from underneath, rather than it being a wild patch of almost impenetrable scrub, to be admired from out.

Despite the logic of removing the weakest, I felt guilty sawing the first one down, even though it was spindly and sad looking next to its neighbour who had taken the best of the soil, and light and won in the race to succeed.

It's a tree eat tree world out there.

I visualised a winding route from our front door, through the trees to the main gateway, and if I took just one bigger healthy specimen out, there would be an obvious path. I pondered and deliberated for a long time whether I should remove it, but guilt aside, it was put to the saw.

I had some gravel in a pile left over from our driveway, and so a few barrow loads, more to demarcate the path than to stabilise it, a small set of steps made of course from a pallet, and I am now trying not to make interpretation signs for each of the tree varieties, as if it was a public nature reserve.

Each letter in Gaelic corresponds to a tree, 18 letters from Ailm (elm) to Ura (heather) (if you can call heather a tree.) I was told once of a wood near Balmacara which the forester had planted in alphabetical order to see if anyone would ever notice.

I think it might be appropriate to label my trees with their Gaelic letter.

In the time it takes to grow a decent tree, a baby will reach drinking and voting age. In some ways humans mature at a similar rate to trees (if humanity has ever matured) and although there are some species that can reach hundreds, even thousands of years of age, trees, like us do also grow old and die.

Our concept of age and time is perhaps problematic and in our accelerating society we seem to be getting worse at comprehending the future in terms of months and years. Of course, time is a conundrum, if we perceive time to be linear, then we may assume it to be infinite (or circular and infinite!) but as mortals our time is presumably limited, and although nowadays we hope for more than three-score years and ten, we are always running out of time.

Especially now, so many projects to finish, jobs to complete in time for the restarts of our businesses, not to mention squeezing in the enjoyment of possibly the last few days of our empty roads and the unique time of having our island to ourselves.

A week is a long time in politics and pandemics. Three, nearly four months is a long time in lockdown. Added into the mix with time, is consequence. For a teenager missing being with friends and peers, it may have seemed like a lifetime. For a business with cash flowing only one way, or a family stuck in a one-bedroom flat in a city, it may also have seemed an eternity, but still only three to four months.

For a toddler, a significant percentage of a lifetime. For pensioners, much less so. I have a theory that time accelerates as each passing year is a smaller percentage of a total lifetime, and so seems relatively shorter...

The consequence of the passing of time and our uncertainty of anything in the future perhaps picks away at our subconscious. As we gear up for the return of tourism and the new normal, we should perhaps take these final few days of what has become an old normal and use what time we have on our hands to examine the short termism we are surrounded with especially the immediate gratification of aspects of our society. We should try and slow down our thinking and perhaps plant a tree...

My four varieties, Beith (Birch), Darach (Oak), Fearna (Alder) and Caorann (Rowan) can be walked through in about 15 seconds, but it depends how fast you walk. I can also sit in their shelter and shade, listen to the birds who have made them their home, and think that whatever I have achieved or not, I have planted some trees.

Saturday 11th July

In search of Skye's lesser known treasures

Although permitted a short drive for exercise during lockdown, we have mainly explored our immediate local space, often walking and cycling from the front door. Having got out of the habit of making journeys by car, in the final days before the guidelines changed we were still rediscovering forgotten places, and last week we circumnavigated Loch Chalum Chille.

We also amassed a final 5 miles for our total of the 'Skye's the Limit' challenge, only being a mere 6000 miles behind the 'Stormyhill Stragglers' winning total...!

The slightly incongruous looking area of marsh and reed on one hand dominates the Kilmuir landscape, and yet on the other lies unnoticed, as from most aspects it foregrounds the Minch and the Western Isles and sits beneath a big sky.

Incongruous also because it is unnaturally flat, a swathe between Monkstadt, Linicro and Bornaskitaig, not an expanse of water, but confusingly, referred to erroneously as 'the loch' by most folk in Kilmuir.

The loch was drained in the 18th century, land reclamation to provide extra grazing and to enable the planting of corn, and also a job creation scheme. Herring-bone patterned drains were hewn joining a main central drain, almost the width of a canal, lined with blocks of stone. It was major civil engineering and construction as well as simple ditch digging resulting in a mini-Suez or Corinth. As it nears Camas Mor, the cutting must be 30ft deep.

As the work was undertaken, various artefacts and items were discovered including two dugout log canoe-type boats, a bronze horse-riding spur, and an ornate carved bone chess piece. These found their way to museums, where the boats were lost, but the spur and chess piece are still on display in the National Museum of Scotland in Edinburgh.

A number of years ago I took a notion to see if our chess piece could perhaps like the more famous Lewis chessmen, be referred with provenance as the 'Kilmuir Chess Piece' rather than just an object 'found in North Skye'.

Perhaps one day it could even be displayed close to where it was found, brought home.

The museum curator was very accommodating, and even personally showed us the display when we visited but needed more proof of its provenance before changing the label. We were told a lot of these artefacts were bought and sold, lost and found, and even though it made the 'Proceedings of the Society of Antiquities of Scotland' (Volume 3 1857), corroboration would be needed. Perhaps we could find a letter or diary entry from the era noting its discovery.

Also problematic was that in 1782 when it was presented to the museum, Lord Macdonald described it as 'being the handle of a Highland dirk' and I believe there is still some debate as to what it actually might be. As yet I have not delved into the collections of the Clan Donald archives in search of a letter or more evidence, but the 'Kilmuir Chessman or Knife Handle' perhaps doesn't have the same ring to it.

Whilst walking around the loch we photographed all the wildflowers to send to my sister-in-law, a botanist who is shielding and unable to leave her home. It's handy having an expert in the family who can name them all at a glance, and it will help pass her time. We found a huge number of different varieties, from tiny white tormentil, delicate carpets of orchids, to stately purple foxgloves adorning the broken-down walls of the monastery on the island.

Clach Chragaisgean is a large stone, unusually situated at the edge of the loch, The size of a small house, I am not sure of how or why it should be there. One theory is that the giant Fionn used it as a fishing weight, another is that one of his warriors lobbed it at a poor girl caught stealing milk from his cows. It could just be an 'erratic' moved there by glacial activity but sometimes a more rational huge river of ice seems as fantastical as the evidence of any superhuman mythical being.

I was always struck in recent years when the endless river of cars was flowing past our house, in search of the social media inspired top attractions, perhaps how much people were missing. To drive round Skye in a day, leaping out at a defined number of tick list beauty spots for a quick walk and a selfie seems perhaps even disingenuous.

The dreaded 'one-nighters' booking in for barely more than a sleep. On investigation during a brief meet and greet, they would inform us, 'We are going to drive round to the Qui... rang, is that how you pronounce it? Past the Storr, and then to Neist Point and the Fairy Pools before seeing Loch Ness and staying in Inverness tonight (or even Edinburgh).

My heart always sank, and I would make humble suggestions that spending more time at one or other destination and driving less, might be preferable, but who am I to curate an experience, and assume that slowing down be a more appropriate way to enjoy Skye.

Rubha Hunis, having not yet made a magazine cover, will never compete with Neist Point in tourism aspirations, and you have to walk further to get there…!

I have always assumed that there is a shared-experience mentality and we must visit the places visited by everyone else, because they must be the best. We can also talk and compare notes and images with our fellow travelers. I have done the same in Bali and India, but must confess, my fondest memories have often been on less known routes when we have come across places by chance.

There is a temptation to judge and perhaps criticise, and does it matter, as long as they spend money. Back in the day when Skye was full, if people stayed any longer than two days, the village halls would have to become emergency hostels, or we could rent out the hen house on Airbnb.

But as post-lockdown bookings start to come in, we have decided to stop allowing people to come for one night, partly to aid the new normal Covid cleaning regime, but also to begin to try and advertise and promote 'slow tourism'.

Whether people need information about their chosen destination is debatable. I am not a lover of interpretation panels as a way of slowing people down. Information is now so accessible and universally available, it seems unnecessary to nail it to a signboard with a list of funders and agency logos, and after a few years of west coast winters and the odd marking from bored youths, they always end up looking sad before they are removed.

It is not for us to dictate how visitors recreate, and how we help visitors (and locals alike) to see as well as look may be a conundrum. We call them tourist sights, which perhaps promotes the two-dimensional. The wind on the face and bare feet in the burn is as much as an experience as curated knowledge of an area. Whether knowing about chess pieces, flowers, geological mythology and history adds necessary value to an experience can be debated, but the slowing down of travel surely has to be beneficial.

Saturday 11th July

Attitudes cross borders as easily as migrating birds and viral infections

Last week, it was with some trepidation that when reaching the junction on the road in front of Portree High School, instead of turning left to pick up prescriptions for Skye Community Response, to continue round the north loop road to Staffin, we turned right.

For the first time in three months, we left Trotternish passed Sligachan and Broadford, crossed the bridge and departed Skye.

Destination: England...

My father passed away last year, and the family home has had to be sold. An offer was accepted, but lockdown prevented the continuation of surveys and the legal paperwork. As England opened up things started moving again, but we hadn't finished clearing the house.

A journey to our neighbouring country and my childhood home was essential, so we drove south in an empty van.

The border...

I have driven the roads between Scotland and England countless times, Scotland has a large blue road sign by a parking place, perhaps to allow people to stop for pictures?

By way of contrast England is barely marked, a small sign, hidden by an overgrown hedge, covered in algae, easily missed. I often smile mischievously. The indicator for the county of Cumbria is more evident, and at least clean.

One late evening last year I was driving this road, and temporary electric signs warned of an imminent road closure due to re-surfacing works. If I drove hastily, I might just make it through. Rounding a corner, although with some frustration I burst into laughter. The road was indeed blocked with red closure signs, and a man in a Hi-Viz jacket flagging down drivers and telling them to turn back. He looked at me with some confusion when I asked if England had declared independence, I don't think he realised the barriers were exactly on the border.

The border...

When I was in Israel all those years ago on my motorcycle, I had wanted to ride through Lebanon, then still a war-torn troubled country. I was advised by their embassy not to visit, but I still rode up to the border so at least I could see a bit of the 'Jewel of the Middle East'. The border was horrible, functional, with rolls of barbed wire and high electric fences to prevent any passage. As I rode a dirt track along the fence, it was not dissimilar to the famous scene in the film, 'The Great Escape' where Steve McQueen, rides his stolen motorcycle along the border to Switzerland. At least I wasn't being chased by soldiers, and I didn't try jumping.

The border between Turkey and Greece had a sunken trough full of water, like a shallow oversized sheep dip. I never knew if this was for the practical washing of vehicles as they drove through, to prevent spread of disease like was attempted here in Foot & Mouth, or was it a purely symbolic washing?

The border into Egypt was more bureaucratic. We didn't have international papers for our motorcycles so although we were allowed in with our appropriate visas, our bikes were impounded until re-registered as Egyptian. This took two days of visits to several offices, payments, some probably bribes, lengthy waits and countless forms all obviously written in Arabic, mostly signed in triplicate.

At least we were given impressive green number plates to strap on, unfortunately taken from us when leaving the country. They would have made fabulous souvenirs. My bike was officially SUZ 2095.

The most unnerving border I have ridden a motorcycle across was actually into Ireland from Northern Ireland (or 'The North' depending on your affiliations). 'The troubles' were still ongoing and I was stopped and asked by a British soldier for my passport and vehicle papers. To his side was a sand-bagged bunker, and during the whole procedure another soldier had his gun trained on me.

A border by definition is a boundary line which separates one country from another. This isn't as simple as it sounds as there is debate as to what constitutes a country. There are states, nations, dependencies, principalities, and a confusion as to how many countries actually exist in the world.

Our own Islands provide a perfect example of this confusion. Are we one country or four and how does the Isle of Man fit, not to mention the Principality of Sealand, an offshore platform in the North Sea owned by the Bates family, who declared independence in 1975?

The boundary of the Great Britain might seem obvious, as a country it is surrounded by sea, but where does Britain stop, and Denmark begin. This might have been academic till oil and gas was discovered beneath the North Sea. And then of course there is the fishing...

During the 1960's and 70's Iceland and Britain had confrontations over fishing rights, known as the 'Cod Wars' or 'Landhelgisstríðin' (the strife for territorial waters). No lives were lost, but Navy warships had to protect fishing vessels and Icelandic coastguard boats dragged wire cutters to sever trawls from the British boats so both equipment and catch would be lost, and they would be forced back to port.

Borders will often follow a natural boundary, like a river, or the crest of a hill, but often they are arbitrary lines drawn on a map. The writer Alistair Mackintosh states in his book on land ownership 'Soil & Soul', 'A straight line in the landscape is the mark of a lawyer's pen.'

Borders were often created with no thought as to people living on the lands, lands carved up by colonialists, the repercussions still evident in tribal strife today,

Borders become more complicated when economies and livelihoods are affected and how political decisions are made.

The day we travelled south from Skye, face coverings had become compulsory in shops in Scotland, but as yet the message in England is still confusing. Having been an advocate of wearing one, I masked up when visiting a store just over the border. Very few other people thought it necessary.

The coronavirus respects no boundaries and can migrate,

ignoring political barriers whether wired and physical, or just signified by a change in tarmac and an illegible sign.

Whatever one's view on Scottish independence and the machinations of a changing devolved power through Brexit and therefore the effect borders may have, attitudes can also cross borders just as easily as migrating birds and viral infections.

One hopes that debate rather than dogma will prevail when decisions are made, especially when affecting the health and well-being of the people and the creating of borders.

Saturday 24th July

Litter is not an urban or rural condition, but a human one

It is exactly twenty miles door-to-door along the road past Duntulm, to Flodigarry and back over above Uig via the Quiriang. A perfect cycle

Seven or eight years ago when I was riding this loop regularly, I started noticing empty cans of a certain energy drink discarded on the roadside. Each week there were more, and I started noticing more. Soon I was concentrating more on the verge than the road ahead.

Sometimes they appeared in clusters, and as I pecked and struggled up the bealach hill, I would ponder, were they perhaps bought each day in Staffin, or Uig, opened and drank then lobbed out of the vehicle window, meaning the clusters would have a drink time, distance and speed correlation.

Eventually I got fed up with seeing them and one day, with a plastic box jammed into my bicycle touring trailer, along with family friends and a pile of youngsters, we cycled round and picked them all up.

96 cans of one brand, a few of a supermarket copy, a number of beer cans, the odd 'half bottle' and an empty bottle of Chardonnay, but in the main energy drinks cans.

We reimagined Andy Warhol's Campbell's soup can picture on the decking, took a photograph and then recycled them all.

Much has been made recently of people visiting scenic spots, woods and loch sides, setting up camp, presumably having a nice time, but then leaving everything from used disposable barbeques and empty beer cans, to their whole encampment. Tents left with folding chairs and sleeping mats, often broken or torn, probably waterlogged, sometimes burnt before abandonment. There is also often evidence of bodily functions during their visit, (the politest way I could think of putting it).

The complete antithesis of 'leave no trace' camping we espouse in outdoor education and try and instill in people when taking them outdoors to 'wild camp' for real, away from the car and the road.

One explanation I have heard is that it is a 'festival' mentality. Buy a really cheap tent which is only likely to last a couple of nights, and leave it all at the festival campground knowing that the organisers will clear it up, with some misguided feeling that it will be re-used philanthropically, or recycled.

Apparently 90% of festival tents end up in landfill.

It might be thought of as an urban-based epidemic and it is perhaps irresistible to blame people from the towns and cities for this despoliation of 'our' countryside and poor attitude to the environment.

However, I have been told of a beach on Skye where recently a party aftermath was left, and only cleared up after a social media outcry. I have it on good authority that it was local teenagers who left the mess.

During lockdown, we cycled the Quiriang loop numerous times, and for sure, empty cans appeared on the roadside. I am positive that my energy drink can collection years back were all from Skye residents, and the cans seen in recent weeks must have been transported by Skye cars or vans. There was no one else here.

It is not just on the land. A gamekeeper friend of mine worked in Ardnamurchan and on one beautiful day on the coast while out stalking, he turned his binoculars towards a small creel boat where he watched with disgust as the fisherman threw two plastic oil containers overboard.

Litter is not an urban or rural condition, but a human one. You either clear up after yourself appropriately, or you don't. It makes no difference where you come from.

One could rant, get angry but to what point? Understanding a problem is a better and more appropriate way of finding a solution.

Ecopsychology studies the relationship between human beings and the natural world through ecological and psychological principles, and amongst other things tries to understand the emotional connection which may exist. I have read discussions suggesting that the way we treat the environment is a reflection of how we view ourselves.

It is perhaps stretching the point to connect the leaving of a tent and barbeque debris by Loch Lomond to teenage self-harm, but if a person has little respect for themselves, then it is not a huge assumption to suggest that they may have little respect for anything else, and crucially, vice-versa.

Loutish, anti-social behaviour and this disregard for surrounding will have roots in upbringing, schooling, role modelling and treatment from society. Deep down, there is a reason.

A reason, but not an excuse.

Ironically the desire to go camping in the outdoors, visiting more natural places, is a positive thing, and often regarded as a first step to creating concern for the environment and conservation. This in turn can lead to a greater understanding of sustainability and the bigger issues of climate change. There are also of course the well-known benefits to individual mental health and well-being, it is just that some people will have to learn to stop wrecking places as part of that process.

Our instructor returned from the first post-lockdown canoe session at Loch Mealt (Kilt Rock) with a bin liner full of disposable barbeque and bottles, left presumably by someone in a camper van. Many years ago, National Park managers in England would debate, do you provide bins which overflow, and need emptying at a cost, or not, in the hope that people take their litter home.

An understanding of rationale and guidance versus legal compliance could be made with the wearing of masks or face-covering during a pandemic. When scientists and health professionals recommended wearing masks in public there was apparently an approximate 5% compliance. Similarly when the Scottish Government recommended wearing face coverings indoors, there was again a 5% compliance. It only rose to a 95% when it became mandatory.

Even with something that is understood to protect the health of other people, and perhaps the showing of respect for those other people and oneself, we still need to be told.

Unfortunately, it seems that our society needs deterrents as much as reasoning and rationality.

People need told, not asked to take their rubbish home.

Whilst it might be suggested that 'society is to blame', fixing the ills of a society is likely to take longer than the fixing of a litter problem, and until there is more education, respect and understanding, one solution is that of enforcement.

Hence the need for fines, although perhaps some kind of community service with appropriate experiential connections might have a greater long-lasting impact.

The greatest irony is that many of us who would never dream of despoiling a landscape with camping detritus, are guilty of adding unnecessarily to unsustainability and climate change. Far subtler than littering but with far greater consequence...

Saturday 31st July

Rediscovering the art of face-to-face conversation

Yesterday I was fixing equipment in my shed when a man, dutifully wearing a mask, walked up the drive. My traditional 'default' greeting of, 'Hi can I help you?' caused the response, 'Can I ask a favour?'

He and his partner were traveling around in a van and their air bed had gone saggy, he needed a 240v supply to blow it up. There on the ground next to me was an extension lead plugged into my power washer. It was easy enough for them to drive the van up and put in a few PSI and make their next night more comfortable.

Of course, we started chatting and in that serendipitous small world way it turned out that the lady had worked with my father many years ago, and knew people from the village I had grown up in.

Conversation. I think they may have been craving it. I have noticed that the visitors we have welcomed to Whitewave seem keen to talk more. Perhaps having spent lockdown with their family, only talking to others through device and technology, to meet someone else in reality and suddenly weeks of latent chat gushes out, although I am not sure if that is not as much me as them.

Even pre-Covid, our activity sessions seemed to be one long conversation. If folk spend hours in a car together driving to the north of Skye, by the time they arrive they might have run out of things to say to each other.

During lockdown, we did talk a lot with neighbours as we saw them on their daily exercise, but as we are now meeting other friends not seen for months, there is a lot to catch up on, even if the discussions, dominated by the pandemic, have a 'Groundhog Day' feel about them.

My newfound friends had hired an empty panel van, installed the slightly faulty deflating air bed, camp stove and sundry paraphernalia and set off from Lancashire to explore the Highlands. Most importantly they had also loaded a chemical toilet. This was a prerequisite from the lady and although brought along to preserve dignity, I remarked that this was really appropriate considering the human waste issues that van camping is causing in popular roadside spots.

Their plan was to test the water, if they enjoyed their holiday, they might purchase a camper van, or like many, get an empty van to convert themselves.

The old Whitewave minibus has become too tatty to use with clients, but still has life in it yet, and so one of my first lockdown projects was removing another row of seats and the fitting of a wooden sleeping platform, tall enough to fit bicycles underneath.

The irony is that in the new socially distant tourism world, our clients are not using the new minibus, but following in their own vehicles.

Having no access to materials we managed to create a fine bed out of left-over decking, supported by the left-over balcony rails. Last week's project undertaken by my son, was the fitting of an extra leisure battery, the 'split-charger' so it can be topped up by the engine and a solar panel pop riveted and glued to the roof. All these additions are probably worth more than the van but will make adventures and mountain bike races more comfortable and homely.

It seems however that there are camper vans, and there are motorhomes.

A camper van I believe is smaller, based on a minibus or panel van, whereas motorhomes have been constructed on a large vehicle chassis, look a bit like fridges with windows and seem to stick out more. They also have amusing and slightly ironic names like 'Adventurer', 'Wild Rover' or 'Wanderlust'. They might also have wide-screen televisions in them, in case the view isn't up to scratch.

They also seem to be driven more nervously by people perhaps unused to piloting large vehicles, causing a little more irk to following traffic as they lumber round our twisty roads.

As we try not to get annoyed when they are holding us back from our important deadline, and try to remember that lockdown also meant slowdown, we should ponder on the motorhome advantage. Along with their size is likely to come a toilet, so hopefully no unpleasant piles behind the bushes at Loch Mealt. One also assumes they could have a sizeable bin, so they may actually take their litter away.

For the tourist in these Covid times they arguably make so much sense, a household bubble can remain isolated whilst journeying around an area, with reduced contact to others.

Except isn't that what makes a holiday, a trip to somewhere else, meeting folk, preferably locals from whom you might glean the location of a precious secret waterfall, traditional music session or best fish and chips.

Or just find out what it's like to live here and what we do in winter.

Even the chance has been taken out of 'wild camper vanning' as there are websites and forums listing all the spots people used to discover accidently or by asking. If you share a secret spot, it doesn't remain secret for very long, and soon enough may suffer from a new-found popularity.

Eventually with online planning and a food delivery before embarkation, one might never have to speak to anyone from beginning to end of a holiday, especially if a credit card automated supermarket petrol station is used.

There are however some pubs which allow vans to use their car parks. In return for the patronage, a meal or a few beers, some hostelries will accept overnight parking. This seems an appropriate win-win situation, and of course there are websites and forums online listing these.

At least when ordering a drink, we can speak to someone, except increasingly there are now digital apps to obviate this. Although this particular piece of technology minimises contact and assists social distancing, they were appearing in busy bars before Covid, presumably to aid efficiency. The days of having a conversation with waiting staff may be numbered.

But as coronavirus has accelerated our reliance on device

and information technology maybe we should pause and remember that conversation is a vital part of the exchange of ideas and opinion, perhaps more so than the printed or digital word, because of its immediacy.

It is part of the glue that binds friendship and community – look how much we have missed talking with friends, but it is also the oil that lubricates friction. Most disagreements can be smoothed with conversation. Debates tend to be less polarised when face-to-face, compared with on-screen or via a keyboard.

It would probably only take a conversation to get a motor-home driver to pull over occasionally to let a queue of traffic past, or a camper van owner to carry a spade and walk a good distance into the woods and dig a hole for their business.

As the old BT advert said, 'It is good to talk'.

Friday 7th August

Print is not immune from lies, but at least there is some accountability

In the cellar at my school was a printing press. Unused and hardly known about, I am not sure how we discovered it. With its metal wheels, levers and rollers, screw clamps and trays of letter blocks, dust, ink, grime and cobwebs, both industrial and aesthetic, it was a thing of beauty and apparently in working order.

A group of us asked and were given permission to return it to its working glory, so long as we formed a 'printing society' and allowed access to other pupils. It was presumably regarded as better than smoking behind the bike sheds. Being teenagers of course we endeavoured to keep our society fairly exclusive and soon our clique was spending most lunchtimes learning the art of poster and leaflet production. Trial and error in seeing backwards while setting the printing blocks, and satisfaction when it all worked and we could churn out simple advertising for school events and societies.

As an enterprise, it had other rewards as we also became purveyors of all party and dance tickets, no money exchanged hands, but we negotiated free invites resulting in a full and busy social calendar.

The pleasure in producing numerous copies, seeing a box of cut printed cards, reverse clones of painstakingly set letters, capitals, uppercase, because indeed they were stored in cases above the more numerous lowercased letters. No pictures, no designs, just words, even if the letters only read 'Disco' with a venue and a time. We had produced them.

Now, a screen is digitally reproduced, and if printed, there is no compositor with ink covered hands setting the letters. It is all more immediate, and a skill and trade has been lost.

When all the print-works became digital, for a few months secondhand junk and antique shops would sell off the wooden print trays, I bought a couple at the top of Leith Walk in Edinburgh, and now perhaps like many, they display memory clutter and trinket. Times New Roman replaced with my father-in-law's postie badge and shells from the shore. I can't decide if this is a fitting end for a remnant of a once thriving print shop, or ignoble. Letter blocks which may have informed of war, strike, disaster or celebration, now replaced with knick-knacks.

The West Highland Free Press is back in print, and its name again pertinent, journalists are called the press as what they wrote was originally printed on a press. During the lockdown the WHFP, with no paper really was free, articles and news at no cost, but online it wasn't the same.

The paper dubbed by some as the 'Three Minute Silence' it's headlines and pictures quickly and quietly perused, to be examined more closely later, or not. This physical paper, I hope was missed, and I also hope that people have not lost the habit of buying their local news. Remember these pages have always punched above their weight as a local rag.

The other moniker for newspaper journalism is 'The Fourth Estate', and these pages by adopting the Highland Land League's motto, An Tir, an Canan S'na Daoine, show support to the land the language and the people.

As a 'free' press however, there is also a duty to examine, and when appropriate hold to account all aspects of 'na daoine', the people, all people. The fourth estate needs constantly to examine the other three, which were the nobility, the clergy and the commoners!

Journalism costs money, investigative journalism costs lots of money, and society loses it at its peril. Supported by advertisers, but not beholden, exposition and comment should be unfettered. When the press is solely owned by corporation or government, it is not free, and neither are the people.

I admit to the irony when I say opinion however is cheap, and one of the dangers of the slip away from the printed word, is the explosion of opinion in preference to fact. Fact is often unpalatable, uncomfortable and can cause the fall of the once great. Opinion can be ignored, fact should not.

Facts are uncovered by journalists.

False news is in the news. The spreading of disinformation through social media, from malicious individuals with some sense of entertainment or anarchistic tendency through to the more worryingly possibility of organisational involvement from foreign power. If information is deliberately skewed, there will be an agenda, often seemingly an attempt to influence the outcome of election or referenda.

Physical print is not immune from lies, falsity and the desire to influence, but at least there is some accountability.

There are proprietors who demand their agenda become the tone of the news, but political bias is usually well known and evident in most newspapers.

At least it is up front and should be liable. There is an editor who will curate the news, and print apologies and retractions, however small, if mistruths are found within their pages, and a paper will suffer the courts if accused of fault.

The internet is more of a maze, and there maybe layers upon layers between author and screen, especially when information is virally shared through social media. This obfuscation is not healthy.

Once a paper is in print, it has a certain perpetuity, and although every version of every website ever published is apparently archived, there is still more of a temporary transience about online information.

Papers might end up lining cat litter trays, but they can still be read, tend to be shared, and how often does an article catch your eye when crumpling a page to light the fire...

At the time of my school printing exploits, the local university had an incredible live concert scene. Amazing bands would perform, and once or twice a month we would see the likes of Status Quo, The Stranglers, Rory Gallagher and many more.

Tickets for these concerts were fairly crude, printed with just a simple font, often similar to the collection we had available in our trays, in a single colour, normally black, on thin card, which was often exactly the same colour as a school exercise book.

The inevitable allegedly happened, it was too much of a temptation for a group of teenage boys. More for the challenge than for any financial gain, again, no money ever exchanged hands, but quite possibly around 15 young people enjoyed the band Motorhead for nothing. Normally it was only a handful of us, and it did depend on the colours of the tickets matching our jotters.

Eventually we heard that some of the forgeries had been discovered after a concert, and that in all reality, we could get into trouble. What we were doing, whilst exciting and challenging, was indeed wrong, so we prudently returned and stuck to producing birthday party invites.

My days as a printer were short, and as a master forger and would-be Frank Abagnale are very much over, however, in supporting the press, the Fourth Estate, although offering opinion, I will always endeavour to seek out some understanding behind the news.

Long may that news be in print.

Friday 14th August

After the exams, will we address the real reasons for inequality

A bird was trapped in my house again this morning. With all this good weather we leave doors open, and it is not uncommon to find a robin, or a sparrow confused and frightened, battering itself against a window trying to get out.

We open a window as wide as possible and close the door to whichever room they are in and hope they find their way to the opening.

One was in my shed, during lockdown, and I was doubly worried for it, clattering amongst jars of paint brushes and white spirit and getting covered in sawdust and cobwebs. We managed to catch this one as it seemed to give up and freeze in terror. Its scared beating heart could be felt while its eyes stared wide and uncomprehending at its temporary captor.

It is horrible seeing them terrified and disorientated. Presumably they are unable to comprehend glass. Solid air, and an open window to freedom looks just like a closed one to a bird brain.

Things are often not what they seem.

It is 'NoWrongPath' time of year again, as our young people have received exam results which may dictate future roads and careers. This year the route to any onward path has been like no other, mixed with pandemic and uncertainty, topped with a mix of teacher and algorithmic assessment.

It was never going to work smoothly as a fool-proof system of assessing pupils, giving them fair exam results without actually sitting the exams. A chimera if ever there was one.

My children have thankfully left school, but one of them failed their prelims fairly spectacularly, so much so, the school perhaps worried about their own attainment, recommended that a lower standard maths exam be taken. This attitude was not child-centred, and erroneous, as with a bit of focus and personal hard work, an A was attained in the real exam.

A common scenario, poor prelims are the stimulus required to cause a major catch up. I believe it is especially common in boys.

If this had all happened this year, the school would have likely and perhaps appropriately predicted an E, this might have been upped to a D due to school overall performance and the postcode lottery.

It would have been wrong.

Our systems are never going to work for outliers, a one size fits all approach to education is going to create mediocrity, and the same approach to assessment will create unfairness and inconsistency.

There has been a public outcry this year, as schools from deprived areas are marked down to be in line with previous year's average.

I have to wonder, where was the public outcry over previous year's attainment from these schools?

The SQA's results algorithms have been accused of classism and bias towards affluent areas. There is outrage, and quite rightly there should be an attempt to fix the problem and help individuals who may have been impeded, but these results are a symptom not a cause, of something far more endemic, and perhaps far worse than any pandemic.

That of a systematic failure of governments to address the root cause of poverty and deprivation throughout our land, manifesting itself as an attainment gap, which is not an education issue, but a societal issue.

My brother used to wear a t-shirt with a picture of a leaping whale and the slogan, 'some things should be above politics'.

Education should be above politics.

Of course, the exam fiasco has become a political football, and a vote of no confidence in the Education Secretary has been called for. This is how politics works, our leaders should be kept to account; however, the cynic in me suggests that these machinations are for political gain and point-scoring above any real interest in our children's future.

The irony is that it seems a similar problem is unfolding in England, where the education lies in the hands of a different party. These are unprecedented times and unusual circumstance and whilst the buck should stop at the top, it is wholly appropriate for consensus and cross-party discussion. I don't care which political party comes up with a solution.

Education should be above politics.

I am writing this before any 'solution' has been announced by the authorities, but the past few months has and should bring into question our system of educating, and perhaps more importantly assessing our children.

It has been announced that no child will have their given grade lowered when results are revamped. A pupil gets a university place on grades they might not have attained in a real exam situation, over a pupil who failed their prelims but might have got an A in that same exam, or over a pupil whose grades are pushed up during this mass appeal.

Did anyone ever say life was fair? This possible grade inflation may however be setting up students for a hard time further down the line. If a young person ends up on a college course too difficult, a higher dropout rate might be around the corner, although just as likely is success for someone who might not have originally 'made the grade'.

Grade inflation is a known phenomenon, and the suggestion that year-on-year there is a creep of attainment, independent of academic ability. This is perhaps due to the commodification and continual assessment of education itself.

With teachers perhaps wanting to err on optimism in predictions, it is precisely what the SQA was trying to mitigate against with its school average algorithms. Statistically and rationally what they were trying to do probably made sense, it is just that there was significant individual collateral damage.

Ironically perhaps the SQA have done society a favour, by blatantly using the attainment gap to try and keep the spread of results 'fair', they have exposed the disparity for what it is.

In truth, we have always known about this. It is easy to rant about the injustice of this year, but what about next year, and the year after and the year after that? It is neat and tidy to blame the SQA and the Education Secretary and call for heads, but will we address the real issues and reasons of the inequality that exists in society?

The narrative is 'jeopardising our children's future', a punchy and emotive strapline, but not helpful if you are that child. The cohort of 2020, like all years, needs support and reassurance that there are other ways, there is no wrong path and that the journey may be just as likely adventurous and rocky as plain sailing and smooth.

By the time my daughter decided she wanted to go to university, her school results were too old, and not recognised. Un-phased she enrolled in an access course, which allowed entry to any humanities course on completion. Her school results made irrelevant and superseded. These access courses are open to any and all. There is always a way.

This morning's bird flew into the kitchen which has windows on three walls, and only two that open, it was a robin, and it bounced from one window to another, but on a third projection, hit the glazed section of an open casement, and clattered out, accelerating to freedom and safety in a willow tree.

We need to open windows for all our children, whatever their postcode, whatever their background.

Not just this year.

Friday 21st August

Why do some folk always seem to sit on the angry side of the fence?

When we first opened Whitewave in Kilmuir, for a number of years we also ran it as a café and guest house with evening meals, and many of our guests would book a full-board option. Alongside activities we would be cooking and making coffee, serving soup and cake. Many lunchtimes would see me return from leading an outdoor session, only to be ensconced at the sink washing dishes, while still in kayaking kit, to then meet the next group without having sat down and only managing a swift snack before the next afternoon's adventure in Uig Bay. We were younger then.

One couple booked for a few days, and it seemed we just could do nothing right. They didn't complain, but were really picky, and as ever we bent over backwards with frustration to accommodate. We tried to engage them, but to no avail, at least their glum faces didn't spread to other guests. Back in the kitchen I was all for asking them to leave, surely, they really wanted to be somewhere else, a hotel or a posh bed and breakfast. Everyone else said no, just keep being nice to them.

When they left, they had written a long piece in our

visitor's book, which still brings a tear to my eye. They thanked us profusely for providing a perfect haven away from it all. They had suffered a tragedy, they had been hounded by the press at home, they were grieving, they had needed to get away. It had been just what they needed.

And I had nearly asked them to leave...

Why should we ever know people's back story, the situation they are in and what they bring? Grief is extreme, but holidays can be bittersweet, they can be stressful, especially in these current Covid times. When tourism opened up there was uncertainty, there still is with possible regional lockdowns and quarantine from certain countries.

We were due folk from Aberdeen the evening the city was required to return to stricter measures. We were uncertain how to proceed, should we refuse access, police the renewed regulations? Luckily the family emailed and cancelled, but these situations make for added stress in our sector.

I have heard the comment that amongst the visitors to Skye are a different clientele. We have discussed the dirty camper scenario, but there are people staycationing who perhaps would normally be elsewhere on a different type of holiday and are possibly out of their comfort zone.

Like every situation, this can have a spread of effect, from the delight in discovery of our landscape and place, to the dismay that it isn't Magaluf. There might be an unwelcome realisation that many of our attractions require either physical investment, you might need to walk somewhere, or maybe a more cerebral effort to entertain the kids while exploring, or driving...

Most of the people seem to take things in their stride, but

we never know the nervousness they may be hiding. From being cooped up during lockdown to being cooped up in a car, stuck in a traffic jam on the A9, and then again on the way to Neist Point.

I think there might be more anger too. Anger at the whole situation, lockdown, furlough loopholes and falling through the net of financial assistance, redundancies around the corner, care homes, exams, foodbanks and more.

But there is never an excuse for rudeness. There were two gentlemen who refused to wear a mask in a Portree restaurant the other night, also refusing to give their details for track and trace and were apparently abusive and unpleasant to staff when asked to leave. One has to wonder not only how they managed to travel so far while flaunting the rules, but also how they work, how they recreate, how they have relationships whilst holding such attitudes and aggression.

As ever I am intrigued to understand why some folk seem to exist on the angry side of the fence. Antagonism is not often an effective strategy.

But it is deeply unfair that workers in the hospitality sector have to be on a frontline, having to remind visitors of the rules and the integrity and possible consequence of their actions if not adhered to. Waiting on tables shouldn't require skills in conflict resolution.

We video called someone in France the other night, and they spoke to us wearing a mask. Staying in a chalet, they have been asked to wear one at all times in the public areas. Apparently in bars and restaurants the police can fine customers 75 euros for not having a mask, and the proprietors can face a 1500 euro fine. Consequently, there is a fairly good adherence to the rules.

There is a second spike lurking around the corner, it can be kept at bay by the excellent attitude of those Portree restaurant staff, and the following of those fairly simple rules. We shouldn't need police checking up on the behaviour of our visitors, surely by now there is an understanding of the protocols, and that there is an unwritten contract between client and tourist provision in how to carry on. My brother lives in Devon, which also attracts many tourists, his local butcher asked some visitors to cover their faces in the shop. Their retort was, 'Oh we are on holiday we haven't brought our masks'

Perhaps one of the problems is that our marketing agencies are keen to advertise that we are 'open for business', and that visitors can be assured of a welcome and facilities, with an inference that it is back to normal. But there is still only a skeleton infrastructure, many places are still shut and just about everywhere is working to a reduced capacity, which puts pressure on everywhere else.

It is not dissimilar to the slightly unrealistic vision of the sunshine and perfect tourist brochure, and the reality of the occasional midge-infested, or rain and gale driven day. Most people do understand the propaganda bias, but perhaps they forget that there is still a virus.

Things are not back to normal, and as we welcome our visitors, we have to remember some might rather be in Malaga than Maligar, some might be on their first journey from a three-month-shielding. Some might have argued with their family, and some might be grieving.

But some might be planning to 'pop the question', which seems to happen not infrequently here on Skye, some might be excitedly showing their partners scenes of old adventures and having quality time together. Some are having the time of their lives.

There are as many different experiences as there are visitors, but those experiences have to include protocols and protection from a pandemic.

Friday 28th August

Think of the future, and the immortal jellyfish

Last weekend we managed to sneak a day off. Since the ease of lockdown and the opening up of tourism, like many folk, we hit the ground running, but unlike previous years with the longer and longer seasons, and practically no off periods, there is a feeling we should 'make hay while the sun shines'. We have barely paused for breath, but as the sun has shone, we need adventures too, and Sunday saw us restarting the trig point collection.

Ian Stewart and Alistair Christie have written an excellent wee guidebook listing walks to all the Ordnance Survey trig points on Skye and Raasay. There are 56 and the publication has spawned a number of 'baggers', people ticking them off on days out.

Sunday's excursion was up Ben Geary, in Waternish which we can actually see from our kitchen windows across Loch Snizort behind the Ascribs. Well we can see the radio mast.

It was quite a short walk, so we decided to drive to Gillen and descend the forest road to the sandy bay at Loch Losait, my daughter fancied finding what seems to be house remains at Oans, presumably a cleared village.

Reaching the sand, we were amazed at the number of dead jellyfish washed up, circular mounds of gelatinous pulp. Not yet rotting, they had all sunk slightly in the damp sand, and from a distance looked like worn smooth stones poking through. Reds, browns, blues, my family mocked me as I insisted on photographing many.

The big red ones had been 'Lion's mains', which when alive are beautiful with huge long filament tentacles, that unfortunately can cause a nasty sting. A wee while ago on social media there was a post warning of them in shallow water as a child had been stung. It seems hot water and vinegar helps ease the pain if there is a bad reaction.

My one time helping out on a creel boat in return for a ride saw me getting stung, as their tentacles would often be entangled around the hauling ropes, which would then be spattered all over the deck when pulled through the winch. I was thankful of the thick oilskins and big gloves I had been loaned.

The common or moon jellyfish, the ones we see most regularly with the four ring marks in the dome are more benign to humans, but still voraciously carnivorous, eating larvae and small swimming molluscs.

The collective noun for jellyfish is either a bloom, a swarm or a smack. Many years ago I was kayaking around the island of Wiay in Loch Bracadale, the smack was so numerous and seemingly solid, I think we could have almost got out of our boats and walked on them.

Turritopsis dohrnii is a species of jellyfish from warmer waters. Instead of actually dying it sinks to the seabed, where its cells regenerate, the technical phrase is cellular transdifferentiation. The animal basically reverts to a juvenile polyp stage and then grows again to an adult. Achieving some kind of rebirth and immortality.

Imagine creating some kind of elixir from jellyfish DNA, perhaps somewhere there are scientists examining just such a possibility. It is irresistible to imagine some wide-eyed crazed genius professor in some castle atop a dark forested mountain with tanks of jellyfish wired to some antennae waiting for a lightning strike, craving eternal youth and some Doctor Who like cyclical continuous existence...

Or maybe I should get out more.

Of course, the jellyfish are no more immortal than you or I. Philosophers could debate with biologists as to the constitution of a new life, a different life. Same cells, separate soul?

Although some religions suggest the opposite, Hindus believe in a reincarnation called samsara, effectively same soul, different cells.

We are all made up of atoms and molecules which have been continuously recycled from something else and so past present and future are all interlinked through chemistry and some kind of immortality.

Without continuing into a deep philosophical, existential and theological examination, there is a very pragmatic point to discussing immortality.

There is a huge problem in society and political machinations of short-termism and populism. Leaders increasingly can only think in periods of months and years to the next election, rather than years and decades or millennium. The rise of populist politics is all about staying in power rather than making real investment for the future. A week is a long time in politics, but just a blink in the life of an immortal jellyfish.

There also seems to be a societal contradiction. our young people should be 'living like there is no tomorrow' enjoying life to the full, and yet alongside a laudable zest for life, is seemingly a desire amongst the young to care about the future with real concerns about climate change and society injustice.

This seems to have been lost in many of our leaders who are in the main older, and are perhaps more interested in position, more interested in steering the ship, than navigating.

Politics is not an easy game, but the opposing dogmas of individual versus society responsibility are becoming tiresome. Knee-jerk adversarial comment from rival benches is becoming tiresome. I find it disingenuous for instance to hear opposing politicians make criticism of mistakes a government in Scotland has made, when similar mistakes have been made in England, by their own party. There is increasingly a desire for cheap political point scoring from all sides. Populism, and maxim rather than consensus and rationality.

If we had a dose of jellyfish immortality, would we think more about the longevity of the repercussions of our actions, our decisions? Would we have the rationality of youth alongside the cynicism of age? Would our debating chambers become more consensual, or remain adversarial?

Jellyfish can swim. They can propel themselves pulsating their bodies and using water to squirt themselves along, but not very effectively. They seem only to move up and down, and not really along as such.

So if wind and tide propels them towards the shore, they are stuffed! So much for any immortality when dried out on the sand.

It is more important where we are going, not who is steering.

Chapter Four

September to October 2020

For work and opportunity – people have always moved / We might not be experts, but we are human and can listen / As restrictions tighten, have we been expecting too much to quickly? / We can still question, but with democracy comes responsibility / If you want to finish first, first you must finish / The sweat and toil to keep warm this winter / Outdoor life, key to well-being / The smartest creatures will depend on wisdom over intelligence

Friday 4th September

For work and opportunity – people have always moved

One of our first ever sea kayak trips was to the Island of Scarp, off the west coast of Harris, some thirty years past. Anne and I launched from the end of the road past Huisinis with boats full of camping gear and food, and we paddled the short distance across the caol. After exploring some of the coastline we camped near the village.

Some of the houses were in good repair and although not lived in were still being used, perhaps as holiday homes. The sign for the post office was still readable and there was a red telephone box, but we didn't notice if there was a working phone. One of the houses had a skeleton of a dolphin or porpoise wired together on display.

In the late eighteen hundreds there were just over two hundred people living on Scarp, but all through the last century numbers started to drop as families drifted away. There was no real safe harbour and the main source of income was lobster fishing, tough in small sail boats. Despite the infrastructure allowing Scarp crustaceans to be sold at Billingsgate market in London, it couldn't sustain the primary producers, who typically were paid the least.

Benefits seemed to be one way. By the seventies the island was empty.

That evening we were the only people on the island.

Most poignant were the war graves, we wondered if the loss of those island men helped tip the balance of community sustainability. It might seem unlikely, but maybe two or three more families may have just been enough to keep things going, in turn to take advantage of European and agency support that came later for communities 'on the edge'. Maybe a harbour might have been built, and with developing communications and technologies a viable future might have evolved, had those men survived the war.

Another island, St Kilda, has been in the news this week. It is ninety years since that island was evacuated following a plea from the residents in a letter to the Secretary of State for Scotland, asking to be taken off as life had become untenable.

Much has been written of St Kilda, the remoteness, the mail boat, the harvesting of birds to eat, the climbing ability of the residents, the parliament and the evacuation. Not much has been said about where they went.

HMS *Harebell* took the last 36 islanders to Lochaline in Lochaber, although a number went further afield, most were settled in Morvern. Ironically as many would have never even seen a tree, yet alone plant one, eight of the men were given jobs with the Forestry Commission.

And so, some of Fiunary forest and the woods below the crags of Aoineadh Mor were planted by the islanders from Hiort.

Migrants.

Ever since people could move, people have moved. When humans were hunter-gatherers they followed food supplies, moved with seasons. When they settled, work and wars would have moved men, families and communities. Humanity is transient.

Land ownership and commerce has provoked movement and migration both globally and in our own locale, from the clearances that made way for deer and sheep, to incoming workers for hydro schemes and industry, aluminium smelters and oil rig construction.

The seasons have also caused movement, from temporary micro migration of the young folk to sheilings on the hill to look after the animals (and inspire many a Gaelic song!) to the eastern European fruit pickers who support the Scottish soft fruit sector. The tourist industry has required seasonal migrants for years. Decades back, a Skye hotel survived its summers with workers from the Outer Isles (who had a nickname as if they had migrated from much further afield!). Australian gap-year youngsters staffed Highland bars for season after season, to be replaced with Poles and other Eastern Europeans in more recent times.

Eighteen years after HMS *Harebell* docked in Lochaline with its cargo of St Kildans, the MV *Empire Windrush* berthed at Tilbury docks on the river Thames. On it were nearly five hundred people from Jamaica and the islands of Trinidad and Tobago, moving to Britain to help fill the post-war labour shortages. They had been encouraged to emigrate and get work. When it suits government, immigration is supported and in the nineteen-fifties, a willingness to move and work was all that was required. Construction, manufacturing, transport, service, health all needed workers, both male and female.

The irony is that much of the worker shortage was created by emigration from Britain to 'The Old Commonwealth'. Over one million took advantage of the 'Assisted Migrant Passage Scheme', costing ten pounds to process, they became the 'Ten Pound Poms', the nickname apparently originating from pomegranate, old Australian slang for immigrant.

As white people left their homes and jobs for a new life, they were replaced with black folk from the Caribbean doing the same. The British government at the time was vague as to the status of the Caribbean immigrant people, and modern treatment of the original workers and their descendants, with some deportations, has been a national embarrassment.

People have always moved for work and to find new opportunities. Covid has inspired many people to revaluate their lives, and whilst in many there is a desire to get back to the original normal, for others there is a frustration with that normal.

Rural areas from the outside looking in, especially through rose-coloured glasses, may seem ideal places to live in a post pandemic society. With technologies and more home working, a home might be conceivably being anywhere, a place in the country perhaps.

There is talk of a new migration from city and suburbia to croft and village. How this is managed for the benefit of all will be a challenge.

It is not just for council, agency or government to monitor and control this inward migration, but also for our communities to embrace and help develop. There has always been movement and change, and there always will be. If we didn't migrate here, our ancestors did. Indigenous people are just immigrants who have been around a bit longer, and they all make up community. It is up to community to make movement and migration work.

If my memory serves me correctly there was still a bible on the lectern in the church in Scarp. I was told they tried to have a service there once a year. With changing communities, and as people have moved both to and from Harris, I wonder if this still happens.

Friday 11th September

To navigate safely you must understand the map

Trig points, or triangulation pillars to give them their full title, are concrete or stone obelisks about 4 feet high, and were used from the 1930's in the surveying of Britain. They were built by the Ordnance Survey, whose name indicates the original military purpose, which apparently was to map Scotland after the Jacobite uprising in 1745. Presumably to help prevent another one. When Charles Edward Stuart raised his standard at Glenfinnan, he inspired many a song and myth, he can't have known that on his defeat he was also to inspire the best maps of any country in the world.

A theodolite was fixed to the top of the pillars and angles and distances could be measured to two close points for a small triangulation fixing, or to two more distant ones to help verify accuracy over larger scales.

The trig points themselves are now obsolete, superseded by GPS (Global Positioning System) which uses satellites, but they are still marked on maps, and still very much the hillwalkers friend, giving comfort and confidence when looming out of the cloud, a point of unarguable absolute definition in the sometime 'hit and mist' of mountain navigation. Often, but not always, they are at the summit of the hill. Nearly always they are a superb vantage point.

Since the relaxation of lockdown, in some areas there has been an increase in mountain rescues of ill prepared groups, and some of the incidents have been due to people relying on the GPS in their phones to navigate. Since GPS units became more commonly available, rescue teams and outdoor experts have continually advised that they only be used as an addition to a map and a compass. A printed map doesn't run out of battery.

I love maps, to me they are pictures of the world, evocative of adventures had, and to be had. My favourite aspects are the contours, the brown squiggly lines which not only indicate height, but form and shape. The best navigating advice I ever received was from a mountain guide friend, who suggested I imagine the map maker with pen in hand, looking through a stereoscope at aerial photographs of the land I might be lost in. What would they draw, would that kink in the hillside be transferred to the paper? The answer often is yes.

Hill walkers tend to use either the 'red' 1:50,000 maps, where one centimetre on the paper equates to 50,000 centimetres in real life, or the 'orange' 1: 25,000 scale which is twice as big, in that the area on the map shows half the area in real life, so can illustrate twice the amount of information, effectively showing more detail.

This extra detail can be both illuminating and confusing. Sometimes too much information can obscure what you need to know, but sometimes every bit of extra data is welcome.

Occasionally the contours I admire can merge into perplexity, along with every rocky outcrop, accurate, but appearing as a blur, especially if my reading glasses have misted up. It is then I prefer the simpler smaller scale version.

There is an expression, 'You can't see the wood for the trees'. On an Ordnance Survey large scale map, you sometimes can't see the hills for the contours.

A bit like following the science in Covid.

I feel our leaders are a bit between a rock and a hard place. What scale map should they use when advising the population? Do they baffle us with every bit of science they have received, or do they simplify the information?

Is simplification dumbing down, or providing clarity?

There has been the accusation of confusion with guidelines for partial local lockdowns and the need to quarantine on returning from some countries. I feel it is not the guidelines that are confusing, but the understanding of the rationale behind them. People dismayed with restrictions use the phrase 'lack of clarity' as an indication of their unhappiness, rather than demanding a more detailed explanation of the decision.

When people argue that it is confusing that holiday makers returning to Scotland might have to quarantine, but to England not, it is disingenuous. The guidelines are clear enough, and it is obvious that governments have just made different decisions, following advice from their preferred scientists. Again, the rationale and reasoning may be seen as confusing, and could be debated ad-nauseum, but the guidelines are clear.

Numbers of outbreaks are on the increase, young people

are being affected and the authorities are again dancing the fine line between health, economy and quite simply keeping the population on board. There has been a small backlash, with some people feeling the need to demonstrate and protest against the decisions made about how the pandemic is being dealt with. Some 600 people marched on Holyrood on Saturday disagreeing with mandatory face coverings and the need for lockdowns. A question of scale again, how big does a minority have to be before newsworthy. There is another fine line which news editors face daily, relevant information in the public interest or the oxygen of publicity for a minority?

Some people are quick to fall for the polarising effect of certain social media comment, which can often be the result of the oversimplification of complex issues, and Covid has provided many examples.

In the mix, we have a virus which the experts are still trying to understand, we have the effect on people which are still not fully known, apart from that it can kill vulnerable people, and be deeply unpleasant for others. We have leaders who are juggling decisions without the benefit of hindsight. We have an economy which is faltering, mounting debts and some politicians intent on following a popularist dogma. You can please some of the people some of the time, but not all of the people all of the time. We have a society which wants both autonomy, and to be told.

The map is ever changing, the scale is vast and has a huge amount of information on it. In some respects, every rock, ditch, bog and tree is marked, but the cliffs and crevasses are hidden.

Some of our population want a quick line diagram on the back of an envelope, others the most detailed chart possible. Some will want the aerial photographs and the stereoscope glasses so they can draw their own map.

I have said before that the time will come when decision-makers are held to account, presumably the next election, but the secret with navigating is always knowing where you are, whether you go over the hill, or round it, along the long easy path, or through the shorter bog. The route will always be debatable but we need to decide which trig point to aim at.

Friday 18th September

We might not be experts but are human, and can listen

Last Thursday a friend shared a picture on social media. It was a temporary sculpture that had appeared overnight on a bridge parapet in Bristol. A teenage boy coloured light grey, in the ubiquitous hoodie, slumped head in hands. Although his fingers cover his face, to me there is an inference that he is also staring at the water. Close and to one side, but just behind him stands a teddy bear, also grey. The BBC website which posted the picture suggests that the teddy bear is comforting the young man.

It is a powerful and utterly thought-provoking piece of artwork, which was created to mark World Suicide Prevention Day developed to provide awareness of commitment and action to prevent suicides. In the UK, men are three times as likely to die by suicide than women. While over the past 10 years there has been a reduction in the number of people completing suicide, numbers are still worryingly high. World Suicide Prevention Day aims to start the conversation and show that recovery is possible.

The same day, Radio Scotland broadcasted 'Six Men', a brave and moving two-part documentary by musician and shinty player Gary Innes. In it he tries to search for reasons as to why, over a period of 20 years, six shinty playing teammates from Fort William, his own friends, had taken their own lives.

Gary interviewed families and friends who bravely spoke of losing their loved ones. One mother explained how her son was always 'full of mischief' and 'big and loud and noticeable'. As I listened to these heartfelt memories and comments, I couldn't get the phrase 'larger than life' out of my own head, its dark irony perhaps describing how a wall of boisterous happy-go-lucky camaraderie on one hand can be indicative of a healthy positive existence, but in some cases may mask deep troubles and problems.

In the programme health professionals discussed with Gary commonalities and trends, suggesting there was not one reason behind suicide. Causes are complex and individual, and one telling comment from a mental health worker said it wasn't 'just depression'. Despite the many varied reasons, he felt all seemed to have a 'sense of entrapment'.

Putting complex and delicate issues into words is difficult. Organisations and agencies talk in statistics and academically which will help understand a problem by objectifying it, but all the workers will know that rates and figures reflect tragedy and hurt. In the same way, we use euphemism and inference in an attempt to cushion hard conversation. It shouldn't be so difficult to talk. If a word like entrapment is used by a professional, then surely a solution must use a phrase like 'be open'. It shouldn't be so difficult to talk.

Disadvantaged and deprived areas have higher rates of male suicide, but also rural areas that might have more social isolation and less access to services. The 'goldfish bowl' lens of a small community was mentioned as perhaps creating a reluctance to ask for help. Society should be mindful of how lockdown and enforced isolation may affect some members of our communities. As winter draws closer, perhaps we should use every opportunity to talk about how people are doing and find out how are our friends are. If we can't meet with them, we can phone them. Sometimes people open up more on the phone than face-to-face.

For me, most alarming was the experience in Shetland, where in the past, due to the numbers of young men taking their own lives, it was almost as if suicide was becoming 'an option'; familiar. It seems risk is increased if it has previously happened in a community.

Consequently, local mental health workers in Shetland felt that a cycle had to be broken to help change these worrying attitudes. Programmes were created to highlight suicide prevention, and the phrase, 'It's OK to not be OK' was coined. Projects driven locally have made progress and Shetland now has one of the lowest regional rates of male suicide. It is possible to make a difference.

'It's OK to not be OK'. A mantra to break the stigma about mental health issues and to start conversations. In Shetland it was recognised that getting help quickly is important. Friends and families will always be there for folk, but sometimes it is professional help that is required. That help also has to be timeous.

The mother of one of the six told Gary that 'There is nothing that can't be fixed' and a health worker opined, 'Big problems can be solved through conversation'.

There were suggestions that men will talk about football, shinty, darts, but perhaps not about other things, and that perhaps a discussion on masculinity and what it means to be a man would be beneficial in getting men to talk.

Perhaps the most important thing for some men to understand is that being tough, 'a man's man', big and macho does not preclude being honest, and reaching out for help if help is needed. Conversely friends should be receptive to anyone who asks for help.

We might not be mental health experts, but we are human, we can listen, we can hug. We can say, 'It's alright to go to the doctor.' Quite often we might have some understanding of a friend's dark place, and a sharing might be cathartic for all concerned.

Looking a friend in the eye and asking if they are alright might be all it takes for them to open up, start a conversation. Nobody questions going to seek medical help with a physical ailment, a broken leg. A mental ailment, a struggling mind is no different.

All through both episodes of 'Six Men', the reiterated theme was asking for help, always ask for help, people are there, friends, families and if need be, professionals.

I think that is why the sculpture in Bristol struck me so much, it was as much the teddy bear as the young person with head in hands.

I think the teddy bear may have symbolised unconditional friendship. It won't judge, it won't be embarrassed, it will listen without comment, it can be shouted at, ignored, all indicative of friendship and being there for someone.

There is no stigma in talking, no stigma in admitting

to difficulties. Gary very movingly told listeners of the last words spoken to him by one of his six friends, a toast on raising a glass. 'Here's to you and me'. Gary ended the first episode with the statement; 'The world is a better place with you in it'.

It is.

If you are seeking help, you can contact the following organisations:
Scottish Association for Mental Health – www.samh.og.uk.
Breathing Space – www.breathingspace.scot:
Samaritans – www.samaritans.org

Friday 25th September

As restrictions tighten, have we been expecting too much too quickly?

In the dining hall of Caius College at Cambridge University is a stained-glass window illustrating three interlocking circles, yellow, blue and purple. There is some resemblance to the petals of a flower, the middle is dark where all three circles overlap, and there are three sections where just two circles overlap. The window commemorates John Venn, a former student and president, a mathematician who developed the concept of the figure which bears his name, the 'Venn diagram'.

I have only seen a photograph of the window. I am not sure how easy it is for the public to gain access to the dining halls of Cambridge colleges, but should I ever be in the area, the anorak in me would make an attempt to see it.

Venn himself called the diagrams 'Eulerian circles' named after a Swiss mathematician Leonard Euler, but it was Venn who generalised their use, and technically Venn diagrams are more straightforward. Their beauty is how they can illustrate complex relationships in simple diagrammatic form, and although originally used to show probability and logic theories, they are now regularly used in all types of social development and relationship work. I have used them for years when running personal development courses with people of all ages. It doesn't take much to get me to draw three circles on a flip chart...

A basic example to explain a Venn diagram, uses just two circles which partially overlap to illustrate sets of living creatures. One circle contains all animals with only two legs, the other circle, all animals which can fly. Humans have two legs but can't fly so would be the first circle, Insects which have six legs and can fly would be in the second circle, and starlings which have two legs but can also fly, would be placed in the overlapping section.

The example illustrates the obvious, and for some concepts diagrams are unnecessary, but Venn's original paper, which I confess to not having read, has the wonderfully evocative title, 'Diagrammatic and Mechanical Representation of Propositions and Reasonings'. It perhaps suggests that the diagrams help illustrate the rationale behind theories or decisions, which is often how we use them in social sciences.

As I write this, there has been the reversing of some aspects of the lifting of lockdown, further societal restrictions to help supress the Covid virus. Media commentators often talk about the difficulty in balancing health and economy, bringing to mind a seesaw, or perhaps the scales of justice statue on the Old Bailey in London. Maybe a Venn diagram might be more useful.

Our leaders may very well have paper flip-charts blue-tacked to the walls of their conference rooms, three overlapping circles, one marked health, one economy, and the third popularity. They desperately want each decision to be placed right in the centre, good for dealing with the pandemic, good for business and commerce, and increasingly more importantly in a fatigued society, a decision that is popular.

The size and importance of each circle will differ and may change as time goes by. Health professionals, educationalists, business owners, self-employed, hospitality workers, all understandably have a bias or standpoint to what they think is important, most important. As the gradual opening up of society and commerce has developed, sector representatives and leaders, have regularly stated how they are working at 30% capacity here, 40% capacity there, if lucky.

The V-shaped recovery of the economy has not had the steep bounce back that had been hoped for. There is a plea for more help, less restrictions, but I heard a telling comment this morning on the radio, 'The long-term health of the economy depends on the suppression of the virus'. It seems we might have to concentrate more on health than the economy, and whatever decisions are made, they are likely not to be popular to many.

I wonder if society has been expecting too much too quickly, and has fooled itself into a short-term thinking, and the hope that a new normal would be the old normal and we'd all be back to normal in a month or two.

I think it might be a long winter.

I came across another diagram the other day, similar to a graph, with self-esteem or achievement against time. It was in relation to grief, but it seems relevant to our reactions to Covid.

Along the 'time' axis were the words; shock, denial,

blame, anger, uncertainty, and the projection relating to self-esteem and achievement was very much downward. Only when the word acceptance appears, does the projection bend upwards. The final words are action and planning, and the inference is that life can take a better turn when control is taken.

Shock, denial, blame and anger are all very understandable reactions but are negative. With grief it is perhaps only when there is real acceptance, that life can return to an assemblance of normality, the new normal so to speak.

It is the same with Covid when new restrictions are announced. We should do our best to understand them, try and appreciate which bit of the Venn diagram the rationale falls in, accepting that it is least likely to be the popular circle, but most importantly accept how it is, then we can plan and move forward.

Many of us were lucky in lockdown, the weather was fantastic, if there was no income, we could reacquaint ourselves with our place and space and enjoy time with close family. If home working was problematic, at least there was an income, and home schooling seemed to happen to varying degrees. We all learned to use Zoom. Life is all about making the best of your situation.

But folk were on the breadline, needed the foodbanks, and we cannot forget Covid killed people in our care home. With the ending of furlough and further restrictions maybe putting paid to the rest of the tourist season, as I said it might be a long winter.

One of the main uses of a Venn diagram is not only the illustration of relationships and concepts, but also the visualisation of a bigger picture. There is always a bigger picture, and as individuals, we also make up family, community and society. A simple Venn diagram could have self-written in one circle, and community in the other.

In the months to come, whilst looking after ourselves, we might need keep an eye on our community, and place ourselves firmly in the overlap of individual and society.

Friday 2nd October

We can still question, but with democracy comes responsibility

Some of our guests last week had originally intended to be in Cuba for their holiday, but were instead staying in our wigwam cabins. I thought it would be a nice touch to exchange the new Skye flag and raise our Cuban one.

We bought it a couple of years ago in a roadside store between Havana and Vinales. I had always wanted to visit Cuba 'before it changed' and to celebrate a certain wedding anniversary seemed a good excuse.

There really are old Cadillacs, Buicks and Chevrolet cars from the 1940's and 50's all over, from gleaming museum pieces offering tourist tours of Havana to ropy jalopies carrying families and locals. Most now have Russian or Chinese diesel engines, the original petrol V8's long gone. Our last Chevy taxi booked for the airport sported a Nissan steering wheel and only made it to third gear occasionally. I think it was probably the clutch that had given up. The driver was however determined to get us there on time, crashing gears and often just limping along in first. We cheered every time he passed a green light and could keep rolling, as red lights involved stopping and the possibility of not getting into gear. We made it.

The bicycles were as impressive as the cars, creative masterpieces of engineering some with cargo boots like oversized butcher's bikes and several tricycles towing trailers. No two were the same. The best I saw had a set of wheels rebuilt with thick alloy strips welded between the hubs and rims instead of spokes. On chatting to the rider, I discovered he had made them himself when the original wheels collapsed.

Everywhere everything was repaired, recycled, reused, reimagined. I saw part of an aeroplane fuselage used as a hut. I want to pretend I know about these things and suggest it was a Douglas Dakota, being like something Indiana Jones would have jumped out of, hens and all.

Music was everywhere, and we really did see two men carrying a double bass along a footpath. When the band played in a small bar, they were amazing, and would have delighted any major festival audience in Europe.

It also seemed that people had time for each other with plenty of neighbours chatting and gatherings of folk sitting on walls and benches. Walking through the down of the downtown in Havana at night also felt as safe as anything with no air of menace like in many cities, despite the non-existent street lighting.

Health care and education in Cuba is also seen as exemplary, the oft quoted high number of doctors per capita and population literacy rate seems to have a basis in truth.

But of course, it is not all it seems, and we perhaps see only what we are allowed to see, or as often with tourism, what we want to see.

The trumpet player in the band told me after looking over his shoulder, that it had taken years for him to get his licence to be a musician as all employment is controlled by the state.

Amnesty International is critical and considers this governmental control of employment 'suffocating of daily life and freedom of speech'.

To speak out is to risk losing employment, and even a jail sentence.

Many people would look over their shoulder before they answered me if I asked questions on certain topics.

There were police at the end of our street one evening and we were advised to walk a different way. Apparently, there was a reconstruction and evidence gathering after a theft. A boy had stolen a pair of trainers. It was a repeat offence and we were told he was facing a possible three years in prison – for stealing a pair of trainers.

Communism is authoritarian, and beneath Cuban society which without doubt has things to be admired, is a darker foundation of dictatorial autocracy, the deep irony of communism.

Societies need rules, countries need laws, otherwise anarchy entails. Our own democracy may be found wanting, there are issues with electoral processes, misuse of power, and we could perhaps question the integrity of some of those in power, but the most important thing is I am able write those words without fear of state retribution. The WHFP would not be closed down if it printed anti-government rhetoric.

But there are laws.

If we don't agree with the laws, we still must abide by them, otherwise society would collapse. If we don't agree with laws or feel them unjust, then there is a democratic process, and there are ways and means to make one's voice heard. If that one voice becomes many then the law makers may take note, they want to remain in power and attract votes at the next election.

If we don't agree with the laws around Covid, we still have to abide by them...

I am feeling an air of despondency, not so much at the possibility of further restrictions, but at the unrest it is causing. It is easy to shout from the side-lines, it is understandable to assess all situations from a personal point of view, I fear however that on occasion, individualism may take precedence over collectivism, and that more people might start behaving in a manner that they think is best for themselves, rather than what is perhaps best for society.

It is easy to see with hindsight that mistakes have been made and may continue to be made in the easing of lockdown and the phased return to normality. There is some debate as to the rationality of some of the strategies, the student debacle, the sporadic testing regime, but we have to give the government the benefit of any doubt, otherwise who do we take a lead from, populist comment, those who shout loudest on social media?

It seems at the moment that there is little difference between the effectiveness of authoritarian and liberal governments in their responses to Covid, but as yet we cannot make effective comparisons. One Swedish epidemiologist being interviewed on Radio Scotland, suggested they phone him in two years time, and he might then be able to say which countries had the most effective response.

We are not a particularly authoritarian society, and have immense freedoms, some of which are being curtailed again. We might feel things unjust, but the second wave and localised spikes are looming. With democracy comes responsibility and as things perhaps get more difficult, we are going to have to act with that responsibility.

Friday 9th October

'If you want to finish first, first you must finish'

I had hoped to write about the Mountain Bike Downhill Scottish Championship race due to be held this weekend at Glencoe. Because of the worry about the second wave of Covid, the organisers were advised to cancel. It was to be the only race this season.

I had volunteered to marshal as numbers had been restricted to riders and organisers only, with no supporters or media. Marshalling involves sitting by the track with two flags, a whistle and a radio (having a camp chair, flask of tea and several layers of warm clothing is also prudent).Each marshal is in sight of the next, so the whole track is visually covered for safety. We blow the whistle every time a rider passes and the flags can warn following riders of mishaps on track, red to stop, yellow for slow. The radio helps with communication and the flow of the event, and can summon medics who are on standby.

Glencoe is my son Ronan's favourite track on the circuit. Steep, twisty, rocky and technical with a couple of crowd-pleasing big jumps at the end, it is also unique as almost the whole track is visible from the car park. One could debate the pros and cons of watching the whole nail-biting progress, or just waiting for your son and heir to burst out of some trees at the end of a forested track. At least at Glencoe there are no trees to hit. His mother prefers watching with her eyes tightly closed!

During a race weekend, the riders walk the track, and many prudently walk it again after practice day, analysing routes and sections. They can take any path they want between the tapes marking the edges, going left or right past that rock to shave off a second here, or set up for a faster next section there.

I accompanied Ronan on one track walk at a British championship race in Wales and looked incredulously at an outrageously rocky section. I was mystified as to how a bike could go through it at any speed. 'Oh, we just jump over that bit.' He showed me a small, battered tree stump which had a raised lip by one of its roots. 'That's the take-off'. He then discussed optimum landing points some 15ft away. If you went too far, you would have to scrub speed quickly and possibly not make it round the next corner (a certain tree was worrying them). Not far enough and speed and valuable time might be lost. It seems to be all about smoothness and flow as well as speed.

The riders have incredible track memory. One evening in the van after a practice day, my son described every single rock, root, bend, berm, hole and jump on a track 2km long. The night before a race they will often visualise the whole route down, going over each possibility and choice in their head. With overnight rain, and a hundred riders, or a drying wind, it can however, all change.

Friday 9th October 2020

Like many young riders, my son went through stages of crashing a lot, often breaking his bikes, trying to go fast without the smoothness. A seasoned competitor from the seniors, a man whose plumber's van doubled as his race van pits, sat with us chatting one evening and smiled at Ronan who was describing yet another crash then said, 'If you want to finish first, first you must finish'.

Winners are on the absolute edge of control, but on the edge, not over it. They finish.

My own mountain bike riding is recreational. I have done a few long-distance races, where the emphasis is on endurance rather than skill, steep technical downhill tracks are beyond me. Trail centres have marked routes which are graded the same as ski runs, green is easy, blue moderate, with red and black being more advanced. I am happy picking my way down red runs, which will still have roots, rocks and drops to negotiate.

On one long journey home from a race, Ronan started telling me about lines. 'World cup riders see lines' he announced. After discussion and further explanation, it appeared that what he was saying was quite simple, the fast riders, the winners, look for the smoothest line through a section, they don't 'see' the rocks, the roots, they don't even necessarily see it as a way through, they just see a line.

On my next ride, I tried this approach, and forced myself to imagine a line ahead of me. Instead of seeing the obstacles, I tried to merge them into the background, and look past them. When I used to white-water kayak, I was told, if you look at the rocks, you will hit them. It is a similar approach to riding mountain-bike trails, and perhaps to life as we barrel our way through the years. The technique worked, I rode smoother and faster.

This is mindset as much as a technical skill, don't look for the obstacles look for the route past, and maybe even use the obstacles, like the tree stump in Wales that the boys launched off, smoothing the path out.

For some, lockdown and restrictions have enabled and inspired an increase in sport participation, many more of us are walking, cycling, running, but competitive sports have been more problematic, involving protocols and procedures to allow participation.

The correlation between sporting activities and their benefits to health and well-being is well known, and many of these have been developed during these restrictive times, but I have missed the craic and camaraderie of the downhill mountain bike race circuit, and although I haven't missed the miles and miles of driving, I have missed the enforced quality time with my son. I know he has missed the actual racing.

For many, being a competitive athlete is what defines them, and whilst one can train and train and still participate, without competition, there is a void.

Skye & Lochalsh Running Club have enabled their winter race series by allowing runners a four-day period to run the course and then register their times. The first 5km 'race' at Skeabost has had more participants than usual.

Many perhaps who struggle to turn up at 9am on a Saturday morning can now fit the run in around busy lives and a few who might find an actual race intimidating, can now compete.

Whatever the reasons for increased participation, I am sure the club hopes for more runners when the actual races return.

We should all look for the line and try not to see the obstacles. We should visualise the smoothest way forward.

Friday 16th October

The sweat and toil to keep warm this winter

This weekend was one of those autumnal tidy up times. As the grass is beginning to die back it reveals mislaid pinch bars and pick axes, and rubbish that has stuck in the undergrowth from blown over wheelie bins. All need clearing up or rescuing.

It is also wood chopping time of year.

I inherited a chainsaw a number of years ago, and for my next birthday I received an articulated lorry load of logs, 30 tons I believe, neatly piled up in front of the house.

I ponder every time I use a chainsaw, convinced that if they were invented in present times they wouldn't be allowed. They are vaguely terrifying to use even with all the safety gear on. A helmet and mesh visor are supposed to stop the chain hitting your face if the saw kicks back, and thick trousers made with long Kevlar fibres inside them are designed to prevent amputation by jamming the chain, before it cuts through your flesh. When I pull start the engine, having sharpened the chain, I am very aware that the saw would slice through a leg, as easily as a log. I want to keep my limbs intact, so I remember my father's advice when using knives, he told me to, 'Keep all of you behind the sharp bit'. Chainsaws are a bit like that, except the sharp bit rotates at 50mph.

Chopping the cut rounds is less stressful as I still use an axe rather than a mechanical splitter, a big lump of a thing, blunt so it splits rather than cuts. My favourite tool though is the 'grenade'. If a knotty and solid round is being particularly tiresome you tap in a pointed piece of cast metal shaped like the Shard building in London. After a couple more taps, and a good wellie with a sledgehammer, the log 'explodes', hence the name of the implement. Occasionally the grenade buries itself deep into the log round and there is a wonderful creaking and clicking noise, the sound of the cellulose and lignin fibres in the wood snapping and giving up to the inevitable. A couple more hits and it hopefully shatters into two or three split pieces.

A friend of mine builds a lovely circular self-standing cairn with his cut logs, like a monument to a land rights skirmish or a pipers' memorial, and I have seen an artistic design of arranged logs that looks like waves along the side of a shed. Mine are just stacked by the outside wall of the kitchen and porch.

Although the chopping is physical, and for some reason more tiring as I get older, there is something satisfying about preparing for winter, stocking up, knowing that whatever happens we can be warm.

Some folk are not so lucky.

The definition of fuel poverty is when a household's fuel costs, necessary to keep a living room at 21 degrees and other rooms at 18 degrees for 9 hours a day (16 at weekends), amounts to more than 10% of the household income. Extreme fuel poverty is when the cost is more than 20% of the income.

Figures from 6 years ago maintain that over 50% of households in the Highlands fall into the fuel poverty bracket.

A lot of people are spending a lot of their not-so-disposable income on keeping warm, and for many there is a stark choice, warmth or food.

There will be more in fuel poverty this winter as businesses fold and jobs are lost.

Of course, it is not just the cost of fuel, it is old housing, lack of insulation and poor substandard windows. Ironically human rights declarations suggest that we are entitled to a roof over our heads, they don't state that it should be warm. Another irony is that those with more money can afford to spend it on insulating their houses, meaning they need to spend less money on fuel.

The author Terry Pratchett through his character Sam Vimes, in the 'Discworld' series of novels, espoused a theory of socio-economic injustice which opined that the rich stay rich because they manage to spend less money. Pratchett uses the example of boots;

'A really good pair of leather boots cost fifty dollars. But an affordable pair of boots, which were sort of OK for a season or two and then leaked like hell when the cardboard gave out, cost about ten dollars... But the thing was that good boots lasted for years and years. A man who could afford fifty dollars had a pair of boots that'd still be keeping his feet dry in ten years' time, while the poor man who could only afford cheap boots would have spent a hundred dollars on boots in the same time and would still have wet feet.'

My 30 tons of logs cost a few hundred pounds, delivery by lorry was almost as much as the wood itself, but they lasted a number of years, I am only on my second lorry load. The fuel for the chainsaw is negligible, one fill of perhaps half a pint, will cut almost a trailer load of rounds, which when split is a good few weeks of warmth.

By effectively bulk-buying combined with free sweat and toil, I am spending less money to stay warm whilst those in fuel poverty are often in Pratchett's socio-economic trap. Insulated houses and big log piles are like the cost effectiveness of good boots.

Those in urban and suburban areas are unable to store a lorry load of logs and will not have the facilities to 'cut their own', and why should they. Most only have gas, oil, or electricity powered heating, and pay bills to the utility companies who provide these forms of energy.

A few weeks ago, we had a guest staying at Whitewave, I discovered he ran an award-winning social enterprise based in Ayrshire. They purport to help domestic and commercial energy consumers make savings on gas and electricity costs through advice and recommendations. Switching utilities companies is always regarded as a good money saver, but to me it always seems a chore and complicated, having an organisation to help seems a great idea. There are also schemes to help with windows and insulation, but not everyone seems to be able to take advantage of them.

And there is always the peats, for those lucky enough with access to a bog. They say the peat warms 5 times, once when cutting, once when stacking to dry on the moor, again when carried home, once when stacking it at home and finally when you burn it.

And you don't need to wear Kevlar trousers when cutting peat.

Friday 23rd October

Outdoor life key to mental well-being

Paul had never been fishing. He was a young carer from West Lothian visiting Whitewave on a respite trip, funded by Skye based charity 'Camp & Trek'. I wasn't party to his background and have always preferred meeting groups without knowing too much individual information. We know some generalities and some of our groups have not had an easy start in life. Often there may be addictions within the family, causing dysfunctionality, whatever that might mean. Often the young people do a lot of fending for themselves, as well as looking after younger siblings, perhaps due to their parents struggling with alcohol or drug dependence.

Often, they have never had much of a chance to be kids, and Paul at the age of fourteen had never been fishing.

We cobbled together two or three sets of fishing gear, rods and reels and some spinners, piled in the minibus and drove the three miles to Duntulm castle, always a good spot for pollock and sometimes mackerel. Most of the group were happy just lazing in the evening sun or wandering around on the rocks. Being somewhere beautiful, with no expectations, my team 'chilled' with them, chatting while keeping a professional eye out on their whereabouts.

But we were really there so Paul could fish, and I found myself showing him how to cast and reel in without falling off the rocks. One section of small cliffs has less kelp beneath it, so the spinners are less likely to be caught in the thick seaweed. This probably means fewer fish, but a bit of tide runs between Tulm Island and the shore. We have often had success when fishing there with my kids, if indeed catching a fish is the definition of success...

I smiled to myself, as apart from my own children I had never taught anyone to fish before, and I quickly had to think about the best ways of explaining things.

After a few failed attempts at casting with the spinner ending up all over the place, I wondered if we should have practiced with a weight and no hook, but soon enough Paul got the hang of getting the lure a good distance out, reeling it in at a nice pace so it didn't skip along the surface, or drag along the bottom. I left him to it.

The evening was spectacular, the sea was calm, it was warm, and as the sun began to sink over Harris, an amazing full moon rose above Cnoc Roll, the hill above Duntulm.

And Paul fished.

The evening eventually came to its natural end, the rest of the group were ready to return home for a snack. I was reluctant to prize Paul away from the rocks, and although he hadn't caught anything, he was evidently content. In due course, the needs of the rest of the group prevailed, and we had to tell him, 'One last cast', otherwise he would still be there now.

On that last cast he got a bite. You could not have made it up.

In all my years of working in the outdoors, seeing groups of children, young people, adults have experiences, try out things, push their comfort zones, be exhilarated, learn skills and be excited, in all those years, all the hills climbed, rivers descended, lochs crossed and adventures had, I don't think I have ever seen such delight on a face.

Paul had caught a fish.

In all honesty, I think I was as excited as he, and as I scampered over to help, Paul landed a decent sized saithe.

As I released the hook from its mouth, holding it tightly, I asked him what he wanted to do with it, explaining the options were releasing it or eating it. He looked incredulous, but I said we could easily cook it for him back at Whitewave, and that my rules were that if you kill it you eat it...

After a bit of discussion, it was decided he would like to try eating it, so I dispatched the fish as quickly as possible, and suggested we gut it on the rocks, less mess in the kitchen as the innards could be chucked in the sea to be eaten by filter feeders or scavenged by seagulls.

Back at base the fish was baked, seemingly a lot of young people aren't lovers of eating fish unless battered from a chip shop, but a few of the group had a small fork full to try.

Recently there have been calls on social media to 'Save outdoor centres'. Many of the big establishments that rely only on school and youth groups have been empty since March, and a number have been mothballed. There have been suggestions that half of UK's outdoor education centres face closure.

Many of the local authority run centres have been struggling for years, with funding cuts due to councils facing budget constraints. Big residential buildings are expensive to run and cash-strapped councils have found it more and more difficult to justify their existence.

It is difficult to quantify the benefits of outdoor experiences for a young person, and although there has been much research, turning any positive data into fiscal argument for a council chamber has always proven a hard task. The correlation between experience and future consequence is just too subtle for the bean counters. One child really might make a different life decision based partly on the outcomes of climbing to the top of a crag or feel better about themselves for having built a raft. There are no league tables on holistic health and mental well-being.

The loss of these big centres will be felt in future years. It is probably up to the outdoor sector to argue its case more fervently, but while residential trips away are problematic due to Covid restrictions, we must look at ways that people can have relevant, challenging, life affirming or positive life changing experiences closer to home. Nowhere in Scotland is far from some green space or a stretch of water, it might not be nestled under a castle overlooking the Minch, but perhaps to someone from Easterhouse, or Pilton it might be more relevant if it is in their own locale.

A lot of activities need expensive paraphernalia and skills to go with it, kayaks, canoes, ropes, even fishing rods, but perhaps these are just the tools, the vehicle to enable being outdoors.

With restrictions existing on meeting indoors, even as

winter sets in as a society we should embrace the outdoors, with or without the paraphernalia. If ever I need reminding of the benefits of outdoor experiences, I just have to remember Paul's face on catching that fish.

Friday 30th October

The smartest creatures will depend on wisdom over intelligence

An old man walks through a derelict building. On the floor is a mix of broken glass and open books, the paint is peeling from window frames, and doors hang off their hinges. The building must have once been a school as some of the walls have erudite murals, but it is now deserted and in ruins. The man looks with both wonder and sadness, especially at the painted faces of cartoon children and spacemen looking out into the empty rooms.

The man begins to speak and has a tone of knowledge and understanding – wisdom. He has the voice and manner that exudes trust. He is the sort of man that you would like to have as an uncle, and it is possible to imagine the children painted on the walls of the abandoned school sitting on his knee listening to tales, spellbound, hanging on his every word.

The man is Sir David Attenborough, and he is in Chernobyl.

On the 26th of April 1986, there was an explosion at the nuclear power plant outside the Ukrainian town, within 48 hours the town, home to 50,000 people, was evacuated and no-one has lived there since.

Attenborough explains that the explosion was due to bad planning and human error. Mistakes.

The scene is from the opening moments of his latest film, 'A Life on Our Planet' which was released on the Netflix streaming platform earlier this month.

Generations have grown up watching David Attenborough series, and many regard him as the greatest broadcaster of all time, possibly the greatest educator. From 'Zoo Quest', which was before my time, through 'Life on Earth', 'Life,' 'Blue Planet', 'Frozen Planet' and more, he has captivated millions, alongside the incredible camerawork of the teams behind each series. My own children have devoured boxed sets of all the series, and we have all watched the presenter age, and amusingly see the fashion of his safari suits change over time. Most folk have a favourite scene and for many it is the famous encounter with a family of silverback gorillas in Rwanda.

David Attenborough calls 'A Life on Our Planet' his witness statement, hinting at the importance he himself gives the film. Using his own extraordinary life and experience to chart the destruction of the natural world, he suggests that the loss of biodiversity, which in turn supports a finely tuned life support machine, will result in the same effect as the explosion at Chernobyl, an uninhabitable world. 'A place in which we cannot live'.

Alongside extracts from his documentaries, including many iconic shots which have become embedded in the nations psyche, he explains how if we continue with unsustainable actions, the damage that occurs will accumulate till eventually whole systems collapse. This he tells us after we watch the heart-breaking sight of an orangutan climbing a single tree left in a denuded rainforest trying to feed from the one branch of remaining leaves.

Attenborough poignantly states that no ecosystem, however big, is secure, and continues to chronicle the destruction of the oceans, with scenes from the 'Blue Planet', interspersed with footage of whaling and tuna fishing.

But the film is also David Attenborough's vision for the future, and although the decimation of wildlife, wild places and biodiversity he calls mankind's greatest mistake, he tells us there is still hope, 'If we act now... we can put it right.'

He lists the main issues, the first being that the world cannot sustain a growing human population. However, as societies develop with both technology and opportunity, there are signs that alongside increased health care and education, birth-rate falls. As nations develop people choose to have fewer children and apparently global birth rates are slowing. The reason the population is still increasing is simply that we are living longer. It seems that in the not too distant future, for the first time in history, human population may peak. The strategy should be to make the peak sooner and at a lower level, by lifting societies and nations out of poverty, and promoting healthcare, education and creating opportunity.

The trick he states is to raise the standard of living around the world, without raising the impact on the world.

He tackles energy. The whole of the natural world is powered by solar energy. Likewise a human society could and should be based on the renewable energy of sunlight, wind, water and geo-thermal, which by definition will never run out, as well as providing a cleaner environment.

He hints at the irony of pension funds investing in fossil fuel development which is 'jeopardising' the future we are saving for. Renewable energy should also be cheaper and therefore more readily available to all.

He looks at fishing, and simply states that a healthy ocean could become bountiful again. The win-win situation of absolute no-fishing zones, creating more productive areas outwith. It is all about management.

He looks at diet, comparing humans with the top predators in the natural world. There are very few carnivores compared with herbivores, and to be sustainable, humans should look more towards a more plant-based diet which uses less space on the planet. Raising plants instead of animals could increase the yield of the land substantially.

Incredibly, the Netherlands which is one of the most densely populated countries in Europe, has some of the most productive agriculture in the world. As their farms cannot expand, they have become expert at getting the most out of every hectare, and increasingly in a sustainable way.

It could be argued that Attenborough has simplified the issues, and despite giving examples of good practice, perhaps he is guilty of glossing over the radical changes that might be necessary. I prefer to think that maybe society is responsible for over-complicating simple concepts, as an excuse for inertia in action.

The film ends where it began, in Chernobyl. Trees have grown and wildlife has returned. If the sight of a city being reclaiming by nature isn't enough, Attenborough warns that while 'The natural world will endure, we humans cannot assume the same', and continues by saying,'We have come this far because we are the smartest creatures that have ever lived, but to continue we require more than intelligence. We require wisdom.'

The film ends with an old man, a wise man, saying that it is not all doom and gloom, and there is a chance to make amends, all it requires is a will. He smiles then walks through an avenue of trees, almost the height of the empty high-rise buildings of the abandoned city.

If you haven't already, I urge you to watch 'A Life on our Planet'.

Chapter Five

November to December 2020

How do we make good judgement when the picture is incomplete / The letters home and the sense of loss that never changes / Perseverance, tension and finally something to celebrate / Why the mobile library was about so much more than books / It would feel saintly to dance again to a live band / From the tunnel the light brings promise, but not yet safety / Making the best of things in the festive spirit / Finding room at the inn in Bethlehem for Christmas

Friday 6th November

How do we make good judgement when the picture is incomplete?

When I was a student, I inherited a poster that had been left in the kitchen of a shared house. It had a series of slightly grainy black and white images which I believe were stills taken from a television advert.

The first was of a young man running towards a lady standing in a doorway. He had a shaved head, was wearing camouflaged trousers, 'Doc Marten' boots and a bomber jacket. A fashion that in the day would have made some people cross the road and avoid any possible confrontation. Skinheads both cultivated and prided themselves on an aggressive look.

The next image had the young man running past the lady and further down the street coming up behind a man carrying a briefcase. With each picture, a different story was unfolding. The businessman has turned and looks startled, frightened. He clutches his briefcase but uses it as a barrier between him and his assailant, because to all intents and purpose, it seems he is going to be mugged.

They grapple, and tumble into a doorway.

In the final picture, the view has panned out a little, and

above them a builder's hoist has collapsed and bricks are falling. The skinhead has saved the man from being crushed.

The poster was advertising a national newspaper (answers on a postcard!) stating that you get different impressions from different points of view, and only, 'If you get the whole picture can you fully understand what is going on.' The inference was obviously that their newspaper would give you the whole picture.

It was very clever, portraying the importance of context and perception to information, and played on first impressions, stereotypes and assumptions.

Today in these pandemic times, we are almost overwhelmed with information. Every device and every screen, every radio broadcast and every newspaper seem to add to the plethora of facts, figures and opinion, much of which is contradictory. Often dramatically so. Infection rates, percentages, numbers in ICUs, businesses losing money, redundancies, efficiency of masks, effectiveness of social distancing, effectiveness of societal restrictions. The statistics of excess mortalities and deaths.

This data is both the product of someone else's point of view, bias and agenda, and a filtering of our own, sometimes it seems we are drowning in it, but it is vital we filter it and make sense of it.

At the weekend, I listened to an interview with Sir David Omand. He is a retired senior civil servant, former director of GCHQ and member of the Joint Intelligence Committee. Using his experience of dealing with security intelligence and national decision making, he has written a book called 'How Spies Think'. As Scotland lost its most celebrated and well-known special agent, 007[2], it was perhaps appropriate to hear a reflection of how it really is in the world of espionage.

Not shaken or stirred, it seems it is analysed. It is all about the analysis of information. In this modern digital age, Omand explained how there is the monitoring of huge amounts of data, which needs analysing. Computers and algorithms filter a majority, but then a person has to decide what is relevant. From this mass of information, there needs to be rational interpretation, to assist in the making of decisions.

He began by a statement which I found both reassuring and worrying saying that our knowledge of the world is 'always incomplete, fragmentary and sometimes wrong'. We cannot know everything, and the issue is how do we make good judgement from incomplete data.

The facts that we do know, or think we know, need explaining, and any explanation needs to take into account the whole picture, as illustrated by the running skinhead. Omand used the example of fingerprints on a petrol bomb. Are they from the person who made and threw the device, or the person who drank the wine and put the bottle to the recycling, to be then picked up and used by rioters. One fact but two very different explanations.

Omand suggests that we should look for the explanation which has the least evidence against it, not necessarily

---

2. Sir Thomas Sean Connery (born Thomas Connery; 25 August 1930–31 October 2020) was a Scottish actor. He was the first actor to portray fictional British secret agent James Bond on film, starring in seven between 1962 and 1983.

the one with most in its favour. Tellingly he warns that it is always possible to find some evidence that appears to support an argument.

The catch phrase of the year is 'follow the science' which I have always been uncomfortable with, as if science is clear, infallible and undisputed. Science is both the body of knowledge we might have, incomplete and possibly wrong, and also the disciplines and techniques to gain more knowledge, possibly biased and possibly flawed. I have seen science described as 'a multitude of debates and unanswered questions.'

Adding to the mix of decision-making is the necessary estimate of how things might turn out. Apparently, analysts prefer using the word estimate over prediction, but either suggests indefinite and inconclusive consequence. We have our own agendas, our own needs linked to outcomes, so alongside incomplete data, is what Omand called 'emotional distortion' which squeezes the rational. Our complicated agenda, personal points of view and assumptions can further cloud already muddy waters. Sometimes we also have an entrenched bias, dogma.

As lockdowns lurk in the near future, as we tire of the guidelines and decisions our leaders are making, we should perhaps be mindful that by definition, the future will be uncertain. There are so many variables, and these variables can only ever be partially controlled.

There is the unclear 'science' which will result in conflicting advice from the experts presenting to the committees of leaders and decision makers who must juggle this advice. They have to add it to economic models and, with an eye to their own political security and future, then present guidelines and protocols to a fatigued society.

The individuals within that society then have to make their own decisions, choose their actions, whilst being bombarded by other facts and opinion from all sides, much conflicting as mentioned above.

Most of us, given the chance, and were quick enough would try and save the man from the falling bricks. Most of us would drink the contents of the bottle and put it in the recycling, rather than construct a 'Molotov Cocktail' and join violent civil unrest.

Most of us will try and do the best within the constraints of our knowledge and understanding, and do our best for both ourselves, and our wider society.

Omand in his interview suggested that it is our 'own demons' that are most likely to mislead us. It is really our own values that filter the data we are confronted with, and our own values that are the foundations of any decisions we make.

Friday 13th November

The letters home and sense of loss that never changes

One of the most powerful and poignant exhibits at the Skye Museum of Island Life in Kilmuir is about Portree soldier Private John Macfarlane. The display is based around his letters home from the First World War in 1915. I was kindly lent photocopies of these letters by the MacDonalds, who own and run the museum. Anne and I spent the evening of Remembrance Sunday reading and transcribing them, translating faded pen and ink script on browned paper into more easily accessible typed words.

We are becoming unused to reading script. Handwriting is becoming a thing of the past and strangely, by having 'Johnnies' letters printed out in clear font on white office paper, there seemed to be a stripping back of time and a projection into the present, somehow increasing their currency and relevance.

His words are still of the time, quite formal, but he tells of day to day living, being billeted in a 'sort of convent' saying that the inmates had 'fled'. He recounts the structure of the day, the food they are given, the weather, and asks for cigarettes and chocolate to be sent.

He is writing to his mother and sisters, reassuring them all is well. A couple of weeks after the first letter, only in a postscript does he mention having been to the trenches, but they 'are not half as bad as you might imagine'. He now asks for paper and envelopes to be sent so he can continue writing. He doesn't need any more cigarettes.

The mention of some 'Portree boys' wounded and one killed has a comment in brackets, illustrating his pragmatic understanding and acceptance of the situation. 'Things like that you know must be.'

His talk of the trenches is as much about bacon, tea and biscuits, chairs and a cat, than of any fighting. 'We never put our heads over the top at all – that wouldn't be quite safe you know.' The Germans were entrenched only 200 yards away.

I wonder how much he censored his thoughts and experiences.

We only have John Macfarlane's letters home, but half a correspondence gives some insight into the nature of the letters he himself received. When Johnnie writes, 'For goodness sake cheer up', his mother's worry is evident.

Socks are knitted by the United Free Congregation, and we learn that his family move house from the Green in Portree. I wonder if his suggestion to name the new residence after the battle being fought, Neuf Chapelle, was ever considered.

On the 14th of May he writes to his sister, hinting, 'you can always send a tin of salmon or sardines when you send a parcel' and 'the shirt and semmit are just the very thing I wanted. I must now close'.

Next to this letter in the museum is the generic letter from the War Office informing Private John Macfarlane's family of his death on the 17th of May.

John Macfarlane became one of the 888,246 British and Colonial servicemen killed in the war, ironically thought to be the 'War to end all wars'. To comprehend such a number is difficult and was perhaps only made apparent to me when visiting the art installation 'Blood Swept Lands and Seas of Red' in London six years ago.

Artists Paul Cummins and Tom Piper designed the work, which had 888,246 ceramic poppies appearing to flow out of a window and onto the grass around the Tower of London. It was vast, an appropriate and effective visualisation of number illustrating the sheer scale of losses, numbers which became even more difficult to imagine when trying to comprehend that over 20 million people died on all sides in total, about half being civilian.

It is often art that helps make sense of the world, and it was a poet Robert Laurence Binyon who penned the words, which every year we hear or read.

They shall grow not old, as we that are left grow old:
Age shall not weary them, nor the years condemn.
At the going down of the sun and in the morning
We will remember them.

The irony of war is that often it is futile. Historians can't agree on the reasons for the First World War, it was a complicated power struggle between political alliances, which may have changed up until the last minute. World

War Two was perhaps more straight forward, although it would be a simplification to reduce it to a fight against fascism.

It is right and proper that we remember the fallen, it is right and proper that we question the validity of conflict, to help prevent further wars and future losses.

We should remember the John MacFarlanes and those lost in recent wars as a reminder of real human cost behind the statistic. Loss is the same now as it was a hundred years ago.

I have a friend who is an Army Chaplain, and this Sunday instead of conducting a large ceremony with his regiment, put out a simple solitary service on social media, just him in a church.

He spoke of the importance of letters, and has since told me that before going into conflict, soldiers write or update a will, have an official photograph taken and it is suggested that they write a letter to loved ones. He used the euphemistic phrase, 'Just in case', words which by their brevity are perhaps as blunt as the meaning they portray. He himself has had to write such a letter, describing it as 'a painful somber thought provoking and humbling experience.'

During his service, he read out sections of letters which have had to be opened, letters from Waterloo, both World Wars, Afghanistan, and Iraq. One was by a young airman killed over the English Channel in 1941, to his parents he wrote 'As a family, we are terribly afraid of showing our feelings, but war has uncovered unsuspected layers of affection beneath the crust of gentlemanly reserve'.

The sorrow is that it took war and death to reveal the

emotions that we all have, and that perhaps instead of a conversation and a hug, this boy's parents heard of this love in a letter. Perhaps there is a lesson in these words to us all.

Friday 20th November

Perseverance, tension and finally something to celebrate

Football is a game of two halves, so goes the cliché used by pundits and commentators alike, filling periods of inaction between occasional excitement at goal ends. Complicating the concept of fractions, I believe it was, Duncan Macrae, fictional skipper of the puffer in the 'Tales of the Para Handy' who announced, 'Welcome to the third half of the cèilidh!'

When does a half become a third or a quarter, and how often as children did we hope to get the confusing and erroneously named bigger half of cake.

Many a cèilidh will have a tea and cake portions at half time, but often this crucial part of a gathering goes on as long as any music and song. With the raffle added and the certain participants who must be allowed to perform in both halves, often the second 'half' may stretch in comparison to the first. Many of us will have enjoyed and contributed to a local village hall get together and they can be fantastic, but occasionally along with community spirit comes a test of perseverance, especially if the cèilidh moves into extra time.

A bit like a football match.

Last week's football match went into extra time. Scotland

versus Serbia became a test of perseverance, It was a game of four halves, and then some.

A member of the 'Tartan Army', the solid fan base for Scotland's football outings was interviewed the next day on the radio and admitted to having watched the match 'from behind the sofa' and one retired radio commentator said he had toyed with the idea of asking his wife to watch it for him.

As most of us now know, Scotland needed to win the match to gain entry into play-offs for the Euro 2020 competition, a major tournament. The men's national team have not achieved such a level in over two decades.

The media run up to the match gained a momentum, it was portrayed as not only a 'must win' but in contrast to previous competitions was actually a 'possible win'.

Media narrative since March has been wall-to-wall Covid, depressing and arguably tedious. The expression 'same old same old' springs to mind as news reports take on a reoccurring 'Groundhog Day' theme of infection rates, faltering businesses, increasing lockdowns, and a fatigued NHS, alongside confused messages and a struggling education system. Not to mention Brexit.

And suddenly there is a football match, which 'we' might win.

The media also fatigued of Covid, embraced the match, built it into something more than a game, and well, even I, who have little interest or knowledge of football felt obliged to get involved and listen to it on the radio.

The phrase 'football is a game of two halves' seems to just state the obvious, but now I realise that the two halves can be very different, and the meaning is that circumstances can change dramatically, often after the interval. In sport fortunes can change in a moment.

Throughout the first half, we listened with half an ear, and perhaps like many, knowing the Scottish penchant for losing were perhaps just waiting for Serbia to score. From what I could ascertain from the commentary and half-time discussion at the nil-nil score, Serbia were not playing well and Scotland were actually in with a chance.

Early in the second half Ryan Christie scored a goal for Scotland.

Ryan Christie is from Inverness, and as a pupil at Millburn Academy, he apparently told his careers teacher he wanted to play football for a living. His father despite himself a former professional footballer decreed that Ryan should pass his exams before passing a ball professionally. Thankfully for Scotland, Ryan obtained 5 'Highers' and could pursue his dream and signed for Caley Thistle, then Celtic.

In Belgrade, it was nearly all over. A few seconds remained, the tension was about to be released, along with cans and bottles all over the country.

Then Serbia won a corner kick and seconds later scored an equaliser. It all seemed so inevitable.

Next followed the third and fourth halves of the match, nail biting, and to my uneducated ears, a war of attrition. The game had turned, and Scotland were on the back foot. It seemed just a matter of time before returning to the familiar role of plucky 'also rans'. In the last minute of extra time, Serbia won another corner kick and a carbon copy and repeat of the closing seconds of the second half seemed to be unfolding. I suspect at this moment, most of the 'Tartan

Army' were behind their sofas, watching through the cracks in-between the fingers of hands held over eyes.

But Scotland survived, and now it was down to a penalty shootout. The team game becomes individual. A single player versus the goalkeeper, turnabout.

During the 'two halves' there is an ebb and flow to a match, perhaps unbalanced as mistakes can be made and stronger teams prevail, but there is a combined effort, teamwork, strategies, set pieces. To then move from an unfolding and developing theatre to a clinical and sudden denouement is a brutal process, and it changes all. If the match was tense and nail-biting then a penalty shootout is off the scale akin to watching the Russian roulette scenes in the film 'The Deer Hunter'.

When the Scottish goalkeeper David Marshall saved the fifth shot from Serbia, there was a slight pause, then he stumbled towards the referee for validation, reassurance that it was legitimate. His teammates had run over to him and enveloped him in celebratory camaraderie, bowling him over in a huge scrum before he himself realised that he had finally won the game for the rest of the team.

It is only a game, but people need an escape. There have been studies showing that sports fans feel a higher self-esteem and other benefits if their team wins, and there are natural feel good dopamine chemical messengers to the brain which are increased with the emotion of winning. Perhaps these benefits are only short-lived, but occasionally we need something to celebrate, something that on one hand doesn't matter, but then on the other perhaps does.

When Ryan Christie was interviewed after the match,

he was clearly emotional, and spoke passionately, contextualising the game perfectly. 'It's been a horrible year for everyone. We knew that coming into the game we could give something to the country'. By winning perhaps they did.

Friday 27th November

Why the mobile library was about so much more than books

Part of the interview process was a driving test. Although it was 25 years ago, I do remember the job advert in the WHFP stating that experience driving large vehicles was a requirement, and an interest in books and people was only desired. Like all job specifications, it probably asked for a willingness to be part of a team whilst having the ability to work unsupervised.

My English degree presumably got me onto the short list, but a familiarity with driving minibuses towing trailers of kayaks meant that I wasn't too daunted by the sight of the lorry-sized yellow van. I wanted to write bright yellow, but it had lost its brightness some years past, and was showing its age. Even so people would still see it coming, like a cross between one of those large motorhomes with massive glass windscreens, and a removal truck.

I was the last to be assessed and had to drive from Portree to the second Braes junction, then back to the centre. It was a big lumbering cumbersome vehicle with many idiosyncrasies, none of which could be learnt or mastered in a ten-minute trial.

When we returned, as I stopped the engine, the assessor turned to look at me, perhaps not noticing the white knuckles still gripping the steering wheel, the sweat beading on my brow and the obvious sense of relief beginning to exude from my whole being, because he said, 'If it is down to the driving there is only you in it'.

It must have been 'down to the driving' because I was offered the post as Assistant Librarian for the Skye mobile library. The job title was due to the pay scale as in all reality, assistant to nobody, I was captain of my own ship, master of my own library.

Over the next days and weeks, I didn't so much tame the van, but developed some control. It was more like steering a boat in a following sea than actually driving, but we grew to respect each other. The most alarming characteristic was its ancient air-assisted powered steering system. Possibly an early bolt-on prototype, it was a mystery even to the council depot mechanics. It had dubious value.

Operating the steering wheel emitted a series of wheezes and hisses, but incredulously there would be a slight delay before the front wheels actually turned. This would be fine during slow manoeuvring, pulling into driveways or reversing during three point turns at road ends, but for the little adjustments required while driving on big roads, it could induce a terrifying weave requiring more faith than skill to control.

After a number of near misses, which could have ended in catastrophe, and much checking and servicing of the mechanism by the mechanics, we decided the only solution was to disconnect this add on accessory, and resort to driver muscle powered steering. Luckily my other job as a kayaking instructor had developed a bit of upper body strength so although each day was like a work-out, it was considerably less stressful at 45 mph on the main roads.

I had a specific two-week timetable which stopped both at individual houses, and centralised locations in communities and villages. Most of the schools had a visit too.

Driving along nearly every road on Skye, and to the end of most, I would deliver cowboy books to grateful crofters and 'Mills & Boon' romances to elderly spinsters. Most would pencil an initial or squiggle on the back page, to mark each one they read. One lady took 14 each visit, presumably reading one a night. This was certainly more than we had in stock, and possibly more than were being written, so I am ashamed to admit, I would occasionally rub out the marks, so she might take out the same book, possibly several times. If she noticed, she never said.

Often, I would get tea and cakes, and a blether. One old lady took the same three books every visit, 'just renew them again', she said as I re-stamped them with a new return date, before being invited into the kitchen for a scone. I am sure the books were never read; it was company she wanted every fortnight.

The pandemic and our reaction to it has highlighted the importance of social contact, and the worries of mental health issues due to loneliness.

For some, a visit from the library van, fish van or 'postie' may take on a more important function than any original purpose, and maybe during these Covid times there is an increased reliance on the brief social exchange they bring.

For some these visits are the only interaction of the week

and most of us require some interaction and in these times, perhaps even crave them.

The importance of many council services cannot be overstated, but I'm never sure if department upper echelons understand the holistic role these services may play in society. Lending books to people is not just about reading, something which might be lost within council bureaucracy.

Every few months all the library van drivers from Highland region would meet in Inverness. We could put faces to names working in the library support unit, compare notes and most importantly be managed by the managers.

It had come to light that most days one driver stopped his van, nipped into an old lady's house, lit the fire for her, cleaning the grate if necessary, before resuming his round.

He was told that this was to stop.

The management attitude was that the social work department should help the old lady if help was really needed.

Obviously, it is not in the job remit for a librarian to light fires for infirm folk, but in all organisations there should be give and take, and those at 'the coalface' can normally be trusted to act appropriately within their job specification.

My experience with the council was last century, so things might have changed, but I wonder if different departments ever have combined meetings to discuss how roles can and do overlap. Embracing and developing the peripheries might end up aiding cost efficiencies. Ten minutes a day for a library van driver, might save an hour a day for a social worker. It might be increasingly appropriate for creative interdepartmental thinking, and maybe all job remits to include looking out for the health and well-being of everyone.

Friday 4th December

It would feel saintly to dance again to a live band

Saint Andrew was a fisherman in Galilee. The story goes he was called to be a disciple and become a 'fisher of men' but as a precursor to this it seems that Jesus may have borrowed his boat to preach from before helping land a huge trawl of fish.

Andrew's connection with Scotland apparently began when a monk who was looking after some bits of his skeleton in Greece had a dream during which an angel advised him to hide them 'at the ends of the earth'. Allegedly a kneecap, an upper arm bone, three fingers and a tooth ended up in Fife after a shipwreck, although another version is that a Bishop Acca, from Northumberland, a collector of saintly relics, brought them to Scotland after they arrived in Britain as part of a mission sent by a Pope Gregory in the 6th century. Presumably carrying a saint's skeleton helps with motivation when trying to convert those of a differing religious persuasion or none. There are bits of Andrew in Italy and some still in Greece, but it is not thought there are any left in Scotland.

Of course, it was warfare, a battle, which instigated

Andrew being venerated as patron Saint of Scotland. Some 1200 years ago, the Picts and Scots were outnumbered by the Angles at Athelstaneford near Edinburgh but were victorious after seeing a formation of clouds in the sky. This they took to represent the X shaped cross, or saltire, that Andrew had been crucified on. The vision also became Inspiration for what is now the Scottish flag.

The Romans had killed Andrew for preaching, it is said he chose to be crucified on the saltire rather than a vertical cross in deference to his leader. This was apparently on the 30 th of November, hence the bank holiday in Scotland and perhaps the somewhat ironic round of dances and cèilidhs.

For the past two years we have celebrated St Andrew's night at Sligachan, at the finale of the SEALL Festival of Small Halls. SEALL is one of Scotland's leading rural performing arts promoters. Based on Skye, their mission is to bring performance in music, theatre, dance, literature, comedy and children's shows to venues across the area.

Since 1996, SEALL have hosted over 2,000 performances via a year-round annual programme, including Fèis an Eilein in July and the Festival of Small Halls in November. Their long-time director, leader, poster maker and lynchpin Duncan Macinnes retired last year, to be replaced by Sara Bain and Marie Lewis, who instead of just taking over and developing, almost immediately had a pandemic to contend with.

With no live performances possible, there were some Zoom concerts in care homes in the early days of the pandemic, but it was hoped that the festival which brings together traditional musicians to perform in different groupings throughout the 'small halls' of Skye could still go ahead.

As weeks and months went by, it became clear there could still be nothing in the flesh, so SEALL decided to invite the musicians together, let them rehearse in a safe social bubble, and then have some concerts live streamed, with the traditional finale in Seamas' bar, Sligachan. The performers were also interviewed briefly, and their chat was broadcast during the concert intervals.

It was clear that the musicians were almost overwhelmed by the unique opportunity they had been given, all of them repeatedly saying how privileged and relieved they were to be able to return to playing music.

Many people are defined by what they do, and for many what they work at is what they do. Whilst we are all more than just a plumber, crofter, accountant, doctor, care worker, shop assistant or kayaking instructor, we are fathers, mothers, home makers, we recreate and live our lives as part of a community, but still our work is a big part of who we are. Perhaps even more so for musicians.

For many years I made a living doing something I enjoyed doing, kayaking, hill walking and canoeing, but it is very different taking a group in the outdoors to adventuring with family and friends or by yourself. In a similar fashion, I imagine it is very different performing music in public at 7:30pm on a Thursday, rather than just round your own kitchen table.

Performers tend to give of themselves, and when it becomes a profession, I think it does define them more so, and arguably becomes who they are.

But then to have it taken away.

Covid restrictions have affected musicians in different ways, I know some who barely picked up their instruments and I know some who produced a video tune everyday of lockdown. Albums have been written by some and muse has been lost to others. Zoom collaborations have been nurtured, and technologies embraced, but for some these technological requirements have been a barrier, and many have remained quiet.

The musicians performing last weekend on Skye relished their chance to be able to sit in the same room as other musicians and do what they do best. Rehearsals and sessions in their hotel bubble, playing music. They were thankful, and repeatedly said so. As I was watching the interviews and listened to the concerts, I felt that for each performer in Dunvegan Castle and Braes Hall, there are countless others in kitchens and rooms, playing solo to phones and recording devices, and not yet having had the opportunity to return to the symbiosis of playing with others physically rather than virtually. SEALL should be congratulated for facilitating the opportunity.

It is unusual for clouds to form a saltire in the sky, but not uncommon for the vapour trial of aeroplanes to create the Scottish flag in the atmosphere. In the past those planes would have had musicians sitting on board, travelling to perform abroad, tour their music to others, make a living and allowing them to be who they are. Closer to home, weddings, and events, pubs and village halls have been quiet. Society is poorer for this, and we should not get used to this quiet.

I hope that next year we can dance to a live band on St

Andrews night in Seamus' Bar. Live streaming of music is all well and good in the context of a pandemic, but is no replacement for a live show, a live concert. We need live music in our lives.

Friday 11th December

From the tunnel the light brings promise, but not yet safety

The village I grew up in had a railway, not so much through it as to one side, but by the time I had arrived on the scene, the trains had ceased to stop and the station was closed. Our community wasn't busy or important enough to keep the station open and the buildings had become an agricultural machinery shop and garage. It is now home to B4RN, a community benefit society providing optical fibre broadband to rural areas.

The railway was not a major part of our childhood conscience, although obviously we grew up doing what small boys are meant to do but probably shouldn't. This inevitably involved trespassing on the railway.

Occasionally pennies would be lined up on the track to be squashed by the trains, and on hearing that the Flying Scotsman was due to be steaming through, all our pocket monies were placed on one of the rails. We would crouch down and place an ear to the track, mimicking what we had seen in cowboy films, seeing if we could hear anything coming, to then scurry down the embankment before it thundered by. After the trains had passed, we would excitedly search for the now thin oval coins amongst the stones and gravel around the sleepers.

The railway also offered a dry way across the river. 'Our' side was well kent, and explored. We knew the farmers who worked the land, often having helped them at lambing and haytime, and we also knew the fields, lanes ditches and hedgerows. Dens had been built, and in summer rafts constructed and paddled on the river. Using old oil barrels found in a rundown shed in the village, tied to planks, they were heavy craft to carry the mile to the riverbank, but floated well, and we learnt how to tie knots and the rudiments of stability and design.

We progressed to using huge lorry wheel inner tubes scrounged from a small local haulage firm. These could be kneeled on and paddled like a coracle and would survive a ride down a small section of rapids. The island in the oxbow could be circumnavigated.

The other side of the river was however entirely different, more of a mystery, steeper sided and wooded, the only flat cleared section had a hut for salmon fishermen. Posh folk we assumed, as they would normally shout if they saw us. Like a forbidden land, it was always more of an adventure to investigate, especially as it required the daring scamper across the railway bridge.

There was also a railway tunnel.

The tunnel was quite frankly scary, not because of the dark or the dripping water, which actually formed small stalactites from the lime in the mortar. It was that our feral band recognised real risk, there was nowhere to run to if a train came.

The tunnel was at the far end of the village, a gaping mouth lined with cut stone. 1230 yards later, over a kilometre, at the other side is another village where there is an active station, and what still is a very fine inn. The road takes two sides of a triangle, the rails a more direct route, through rather than round or over the hill, and as I have since found out, a shorter walk for teenagers going to the pub.

My brother is older than I, and while we were building dens and rafts, he was discovering the delights of local hostelries, but it was only very recently that he told me about taking shortcuts through the tunnel. He has since recounted how they quite often used to walk along the tracks, but only ever on the way there, never on the way back, reasoning that it perhaps wasn't the most sensible journey, and even less so if a little clouded with alcohol.

There were not many trains, but one evening despite their infrequency, the inevitable happened, and they were caught out.

My brother says it was one of the most terrifying experiences he has ever had, two of them managed to find a cubby hole in the side of the tunnel wall, perhaps designed for such a purpose. As the carriages rushed by, the pair were convinced the other boy, having run off, would end up mutilated and dead, he however had lain down at the edge of the gravel close to the side wall and made himself as thin as possible. It was thin enough.

They never went through the tunnel again.

UK Health Secretary Matt Hancock said today there was 'light at the end of the tunnel'. This morning 90-year-old Margaret Keenen became the first person to be given the

Pfizer/BioNTech vaccine as part of the largest mass vaccination programme ever to be rolled out in Britain. 800,000 doses in the immediate batch, with a view to inoculating 4 million in the coming weeks.

Typically, some UK politicians have continued using the language of warfare, dubbing it 'V Day'. V for vaccine, but perhaps a thinly veiled V for victory to help bolster populism and support. The second person to be administered the jab according to the BBC was 81-year-old William Shakespeare. It may have been a case of ladies first, but perhaps it would have given rise to too many puns in the newspapers had Mr Shakespeare had gone first. (A 'Comedy of Errors' perhaps.)

Professor Jason Leitch, the Scottish National Clinical Director brought a Scottish air of realism to 'V Day' when announcing, 'I'm trying not to get over excited because we don't have that many vials of the actual drug'. Running concurrently with the continued, albeit reducing restrictions is a massive logistical exercise to actually get the vaccine to the populace.

We are not out of the tunnel yet, mask-wearing and protocols are likely to be with us for a time yet and adherence may begin to wane as the inoculations spread.

Prime Minister Johnston seems to fancy himself as a Churchillian style orator, perhaps we should all remember the famous lines spoken just halfway through the war; 'Now this is not the end. It is not even the beginning of the end. But it is, perhaps, the end of the beginning.'

We are further down the line, but I worry that the light at the end of the tunnel is possibly the oncoming Brexit train...

Friday 18th December

Making the best of things in the festive spirit

The man in the Hi-Viz jacket signaled us into a back-row parking slot with all the skill and aplomb of a 'Cal-Mac' deckhand, aiding our maneuvering with hand signals and a smile. Although emanating from adults, the excitement in the front row seats of my van was tantamount to a bus ride on a school trip. The occasion, a drive-in pantomime at the Sligachan Hotel last weekend.

My kids have grown up, so we have no real excuse to go to a panto, but I have always maintained that the mark of having grown up, is the realisation that there is no such thing. My children weren't with us to feign embarrassment or pour scorn and I could revert to childish ways.

Pantomime has apparently developed from 16th Century Italian and European comedic theatre, medieval mummers plays, and more recently music hall variety, now having evolved into a staple family theatrical experience over Christmas and January. Normally based on traditional fairy tales and classic children's stories they have similar themes and conventions, often involving a quest or search to save an entrapped young heroine from a wicked family member and an animal character who assists the leading hero, who is played by a woman dressed as a boy. It is said that this allowed Victorian male audience members the sight 'of a well-turned ankle'. Perhaps in a drive for cross-dressing equality, the mother of the hero is normally played by a man.

Other modern traditional aspects, if that isn't a contradiction, are the references to blockbuster films, current or local issues, the re-wording of songs, audience participation and innuendo. There is always an attempt to provide risqué humour for adults on top of childish slapstick, although I can't imagine the bawdy puns going over the heads of many youngsters nowadays. It is more likely to be the other way around.

Rapunzel was performed by a professional crew, including local actors Harry Partridge and Sam Smith and young dancers from the Island. The stage was a flatbed lorry, and the show was directed by Daniel Cullen who has run local drama clubs and projects.

Being a drive-in experience, the audience participation was through the honking of car horns and flashing of headlights and indicators. Hazard warning lights had the extra and very useful effect of attracting waiting staff who would bring mulled wine and snacks. Sound was provided through your vehicle's radio by tuning into a specific frequency.

A few well-known local people were ribbed, social distancing used as a joke between 'Dame Donuts' and Ramsbottom' and Dominic Cummings' infamous car journey was made fun of. Apparently, there are dark places in the Tongadale Hotel which is presumably and ironically the sign of a good establishment.

We also had to dance and sing to the new Scottish national anthem 'Yes sir I can boogie', while filming ourselves on phones to be uploaded on social media for the chance of a prize. Due to being swathed in blankets, this proved less effective in our vehicle than it perhaps could have been. Hopefully our noise and enthusiasm made up for lack of movement. During a rendition of Runrig's 'Every River', we waved our phone torches out of the windows in the modern form of the old Zippo cigarette lighter concert tribute. The song was perfectly chosen because of the line 'You ask me to believe in magic'. We sang our hearts out, more so being in the privacy of our own theatre box, and because as this year nears its end, society is need of a bit of magic.

The last 10 months have been reminiscent of a pantomime, the pandemic narrative has been like some wicked darkness descending and enveloping the land. There are heroes, key workers and essential ordinary people who have carried on doing their best, illustrating the normality of heroism and altruism. It is irresistible to portray certain politicians as dame-like buffoons and there has been a quest for a vaccine, as well as many inner struggles.

A main struggle has perhaps been between the desire for normality whilst living in restricted times, following sometimes seemingly irrational guidelines, and juggling our behaviours between what we think is best for ourselves, and what others think is best for society. It is like the hero arriving at a ravine crossing with an ancient rotting rope bridge, and faced with a choice, go over or go around.

The organisers and team who put on last week's show are to be congratulated, they are exemplars of adaptation and turning negatives into positives. There will always be people who make things happen, it is part of human and community spirit, movers and shakers come in all guises, a nurse's uniform, or the striped suit of a pantomime character, the Hi-Viz of a volunteer in a safety jacket, or a local tradesman who provides enabling funds. It is both the making the best of a situation, and the turning of that situation into a positive. Importantly it is a realisation that perhaps something can be made better than before.

For some, the recent months have been more tragic than pantomime with loss of income and financial hardship, or a real feeling of entrapment. Rapunzel was not only supporting the health and well-being of a community by putting on a show, providing much needed live entertainment, they were also supporting the local food bank.

Driving away, we passed a man carrying jump leads, I had wondered if all the honking and flashing might be too much for some vehicle batteries, but help was at hand for any car not starting.

We decided to take a run through the village, primarily to look at the Christmas lights, both in the main streets and round the houses. As usual, the road up to the Home Farm care home didn't disappoint, and if anywhere needs a dose of Christmas cheer it is the local care home, who have had such a difficult year.

There seem to be more lights around houses this year, perhaps an indication that this year we need a bit more brightness.

Pantomime stories although dressed up with double entendre, horseplay and joke are always about good triumphing over evil. The wicked witch is always defeated, banished or better still transformed after realising the error of their ways. On Saturday night, all we had to do was flash our headlights and the enchantress who had locked Rapunzel in the tower, changed her wicked ways, and announced how good it felt.

All we have to do is light up people's lives, perhaps it really is that easy.

Friday 25th December

Finding room at the inn for Christmas in Bethlehem

It was forbidden to take fruit across the border, but because our oranges were about to be confiscated, Mike pleaded, 'Can we not eat them?' The Israeli customs guard gave us a bemused 'I suppose so' shrug, so while he was searching our dirty oily sand-covered motorbikes and rifling through the grimy bags for bombs or contraband, we munched through our supplies.

Having practically run out of money, the thought of throwing away good food was an anathema especially as we had stocked up in Egypt, correctly presuming it to be cheaper than Israel.

The plan, somewhat naïve and really just a vague idea, was to stay on a kibbutz, but it was only the next day we learned of the six-month waiting list and the required agency letter of introduction.

Not being able to camp in the city of Tel Aviv, we had discovered a semi-derelict building, with steel reinforcing bars jutting out from the edges of the concrete floors and an open stairway between support pillars, no bannisters, no doors and perfect for our needs. We could keep an eye on the bikes in the street, as not only were there no windows, there were no walls. Most importantly it was free.

The kibbutz office put us on to another organisation which might be able to help. A moshav was described as being similar to a kibbutz but with no facilities, no swimming pool, no bar, no gym, basically just a work camp. The moshav office was like a social work drop-in centre for broke itinerants and lost travellers run by a plump lady called Meira who doubled as a mother hen. Most welcome was the coffee and biscuits which were freely available. The biggest concern to Meira was our motorcycles. Having left them at our dilapidated lodgings she was convinced that our bags would either be stolen or blown up by the army. Luckily neither happened.

Despite being well down in the queue, perhaps our charm, or fairly dire situation meant we were offered a place at Na'ama, a new camp near Jericho. As we left the office with raised spirits, and the opening of new chapter to our adventure, a man in the room looked at us and announced, 'Na'ama, it is the worst Moshav in Israel, nobody lasts'.

We did.

In the weeks running up to Christmas, I was picking bananas on the West Bank in the Jordan Valley. Mike picked aubergines and dates. The farmers were kind, but expected hard work. The other workers were mostly in a similar position to ourselves, broke and a long way from home. Some were saving for a flight back, others running away, never intending to return.

Having a couple of days off for Christmas, I hitch-hiked to Jerusalem with a plan to visit the sites and investigate getting to Bethlehem. Mike and some of our new-found friends would join me on Christmas Eve.

The centre of Bethlehem, a short bus ride away from Jerusalem, was cordoned off with a large high metal fence, and people were searched before entering, under the watchful eye of a soldier standing statue like on sandbags with an automatic rifle. There was a square with a Christmas tree, a string of coloured lights, and lots of people milling about.

The Church of the Nativity has been built on the spot where it is believed that Jesus was born. There is some scholarly discussion as to whether this was a cave, a stable, or perhaps the most likely, a back room off a house which housed both people and beasts. Common in rural peasant communities, not dissimilar from the black houses here, it is not inconceivable that his birthplace was a combination of all these things as caves and rock overhangs have long been adapted for storage and extensions to buildings. Language, translation and semantics can add a lens to history, which can be both insightful and opaque. There is a grotto in the church which is supposedly the exact place of Jesus' birth and is the oldest site continuously used as a place of Christian worship.

There was no way we were going to get near the church, there were too many people, and my idea of attending a midnight mass was definitely not an option. We would have had to be in place hours before, and I heard that tickets were necessary.

Christmas Eve 1985 was therefore spent in a bar close to the place where Jesus might have been born.

It was probably more appropriate, after a few drinks

Mike and I could sing and shout, laugh and cry, hug each other and feel some sense of achievement. We had made it, we had ridden our motorcycles to Israel. What had started off as an idle idea, became a seed which had grown into a plan resulting in a life-changing experience.

We had broken down, fallen off, got lost, seen incredible things, run out of money, and shared amazing times, both good and not so good.

Above all, we had met people and we had been showed kindness, from Jew, Arab, Christian and atheist.

The banana farmer near Jericho who looked after us in Na'ama was no different from the Syrian school teacher who shared a meal with us, who was no different from the Serbian labourer and his family, with whom we spent a wild night. The Greek mechanic who helped fix a buckled wheel (long story) and the Muslim who tried to teach me both backgammon and the words to the Adhan, the Islamic call to prayer.

People who showed kindness to and shared time with two grubby foreign motorcyclists.

Christmas is a Christian festival that through faith, belief and story morphed a pagan winter ceremony into a worldwide phenomenon. Both commercialism and secularism have perhaps taken it somewhere else, but for many, for most, there is still a message. Christians rightly concentrate on the spread of their specific faith, but surely the most important aspect of that message overlaps other beliefs and none. For me the message is not about belief or faith, it is quite simply the spread of love and kindness to all.

Merry Christmas.

Chapter Six

January to February 2021

Looking back to look forward to a new year / Lorna showed that bravery can take many forms / First taste of Burns became a test of character / Run jump slide and skid – let the urge take hold / Turning skill and passion into real entertainment / We are taught but only from our own mistakes do we learn / Relief at the rain as 'controlled burning' gets out of hand / As simple and powerful as flicking a switch

Friday 8th January

Looking back to look forward to a new year

The origin of the word Hogmanay is uncertain, perhaps coming from the Norman French 'Hoguinane', or the Old French 'Aguillanneuf', meaning the last day of the year and a New Year's Eve gift. The French word for mistletoe, 'du gui' might also be involved in the etymology. Whilst Scotland is famous for celebrating year ends, customs don't respect borders, in Yorkshire and Cumbria, 'Hagman-heigh' or 'Hogmina' were also toasted.

But we do it best here.

Having a quiet evening up until 'the bells' with the family, and then the anticipation of what might happen next was always great craic. If the night was clear and starlit, there would be promise of visitors or visiting, which when we were 'young and fun to be with' could go on for days. One infamous year, we took our baby daughter around the neighbours and relatives, pushing her in the pram, which also doubled as useful transport for the ubiquitous bottle (or bottles!) of whisky. Our child was eventually kidnapped by an old auntie who refused to let us navigate the pushchair home along the road, worrying that we would all end up capsized in a ditch, 'I'll look after her, you go straight home to bed,' she decreed. After the inevitable protestations and pretence at being responsible parents, we agreed, and of course being unencumbered managed several more visits and drams before the morning dawned. I think the daughter was repatriated at some point later on that day. It might have been the next...

Traditions change, and the irony is that Scotland has become best known for a more modern interpretation of bringing in the new, that of the big street party and firework display, for which Edinburgh is exemplary. 2019 saw us visiting the now grown-up daughter who seemingly survived her infantile first footing escapades on Skye and lives in Leith. We enjoyed the massed fire torch procession at the start of the festival and reveled in being in the city. Princes Street had been closed to traffic, and as the shops were shutting on the 31st itself, the street was strangely empty, most people saving themselves for the big party. I relished walking down the middle of the traffic-free road. Who would have known that the streets would again be empty for a more serious reason just three months later?

New Year is a time for looking in all directions, past, present and future. The narrative for 2020 was negative, most social media messages have been hoping for a better year, for many there has been loss, sadness, worry and stress, both health and financial. There has been frustration, restriction and forced separation. But we shouldn't forget that along with restriction came kindness, opportunity and time, time to spend with family, time to explore our place and time to be kind to others. It wasn't all bad, and we could not have asked for better weather during the first lockdown.

This week has seen more restrictions, almost a return to the original lockdown, a second wave has manifest into a new variant. Here we go again. Pre-Christmas, the decision makers were between the devil and the deep blue sea, dancing the line between popularism, pragmatism, health, education and economy, allowing a relaxation of restrictions because it would happen anyway. The strategy was perhaps to allow a little to prevent a lot. The result, probably a post-Christmas wave, but hopefully less than it could have been. Thank goodness there is a vaccine.

Looking back to look forward. Two of my oldest friends helped me with a project this year, guys I met over 30 years ago when I first moved to Skye, there are now children, even grandchildren, and reference was made to 'The Last of the Summer Wine', all good fun except I think I was meant to be the character 'Compo'.

Each of us voted differently in the past two referenda, we were the complete spread of opinion and spectrum. In the past, there has been the odd heated discussion and we have agreed to differ, we are still friends. Debate discuss, argue, disagree, but always remain respectful. The scourge of social media, populist politicking and the polarisation of dogma is that entrenched views and unwavering attitudes can manifest themselves into vitriol.

For 2021 we could do with more empathy in the world, and I think the next months, even years may be tough, remaining respectful with those with whom we disagree can only help.

This year's Edinburgh Hogmanay was marked by a series

of three short films based around the poem 'Fare Well' by Scots poet Jackie Kay, read out by a collection of folk including Winnie Brook Young and Lorne MacFadyen from Skye. Fireworks were replaced by an incredible swarm of drones, each carrying a light, and choreographed by computer to dance in the sky, forming words, semiotic shapes and symbols. These were filmed in the Highlands, but also merged into iconic Scottish views.

The first part was a look back at the year gone by, the funerals and weddings cancelled, the poignant line describing social distancing, 'The Saltire's been a warning cross. Dinny come too near'. The second film reflected on human spirit and the sense of togetherness which has emerged, 'and now we ken oor neighbours' names... we send emojis through the ether, to weather the storm; together, alone.' The final show was a message of hope, 'We share the planet's air. What's yours is mine...'

The music for the films was composed by the Skye band Niteworks. The island has always punched above its weight in the creative industries, and it is encouraging to see that this is still evident in these uncertain times.

The dancing drone display was appropriate and beautiful, and the messages spelled out in the sky simple and succinct. The films are still available to watch online. If you haven't watched them, I urge you to find them on the internet, sit in a comfortable chair, next to someone you love if you can and by a fire if you have one, perhaps with a small dram and press play.

We have looked back, and looked forward, it is also appropriate to look up.

There ur seeds on the air which will be trees.
Choreography on the air, danced by bees.
There's auld licht made braw by a billion stars;
The pure white o Venus an the red o Mars

The drones rose above the bridges over the Forth and wrote in the sky:

WE ARE ONE
2021

Bliadhna Mhath Ùr

Friday 15th January

Lorna showed that bravery can take many forms

Brave is a word we often think of in relation to an act or a feat, something done on a battlefield by a soldier in the line of fire, or a by person who puts themselves in danger, perhaps taking a risk in order to save a life.

Often bravery is when ordinary people do extraordinary things. These may be the quick instinctive responses to prevent harm, perhaps done with little or no thought to possible personal consequence, but might also be the measured altruistic choice of putting others before oneself. There are other forms of bravery.

Bravery can also be mixed in with tenacity and resilience, a human spirit to continue in the face of adversity, the marathon of managing an unchanging or slow unfolding situation, rather than the sprint to save a stranger from falling scaffolding. A way of being rather than the consequence of a single event.

For many brave people, the extraordinary thing might just be coping with the adversity of circumstance, and the circumstance might be day-to-day living with a debilitating medical condition.

Lipoedema is thought to affect around 300,000 women in Scotland. It is a genetic disorder where there is a disproportionate accumulation of weight around the middle of the body due to abnormal fat cells. The impact is not only on mobility and appearance, but obviously on general wellbeing and state of mind.

'Lipoedema – Sgeulachd Lorna', is the story of Lorna Taggart from Skye who has had to deal with the condition all her adult life. Shown last week on BBC ALBA the film charts her journey from teens through to the current time, and is a poignant and moving documentary, filmed by her brother, the broadcaster John McDiarmid.

We join her in a normality of life, the long commute to Sleat to teach at the school, the visit to the music festival where she camps with her family, her life living in a caravan, like so many waiting for a house to be built, to be finished.

But then we also witness the toll of this normality, her pain, her exhaustion, the effort required, barely being able to move after her drive from school, collapsing in her tent at the festival and missing her favourite band. At times, it seems everything is a massive undertaking requiring perseverance and tenacity.

One of the issues with Lipoedema is that it is poorly understood by both the medical profession and society. We see overweight people, obese people and there is perhaps a tendency to think that it is the result of lifestyle, bad diet, lack of exercise, self-inflicted.

Lipoedema is a medical condition. In a survey of women with Lipoedema, despite developing symptoms between the ages of 18-25, only 7% were diagnosed and most took decades to realise they had the condition and were routinely dismissed by doctors and nurses, often being told that the excess fat 'was their own fault'. It isn't.

Lorna suffered bullying at school when young, and her father's frustration at her size. A major sadness was her father passing away without ever knowing that it wasn't her fault.

There is no cure for Lipoedema, only ways of managing it. We go with Lorna to a national conference where she meets other women who have it. We see a funny short phone video of compression tights, there is laughter and an understanding. There is a chance to buy clothes. At the conference, there is a presentation about liposuction, a fat-removing surgical procedure, which has the potential to alleviate debilitation and possibly transform their lives. Unfortunately, the NHS considers liposuction as a cosmetic procedure, so it is only rarely available. Alex Munnoch the surgeon from Ninewells hospital in Dundee. who can in some cases offer liposuction through the NHS admits that he is the only option in Scotland.

Lorna is put forward for the operation, but has to lose some weight, and we are with her when the letter arrives and she phones her mother to tell her the news, she has been accepted for the procedure, there are tears. But alongside this news is the journey to Ninewells and the consultant to discover the condition, which is genetic, has also passed to her daughter.

Then Covid hits.

Lorna has been expecting the phone call which postpones her procedure. The filming changes to a phone video diary, and we can detect the frustration, the toll of the dashed hope on top of the strains of her everyday living, on top of lockdown. We see this strong amazing woman at her lowest, now back in limbo, not knowing when or if this life changing operation will ever happen.

I have regularly tried to remain upbeat about the pandemic and its effects, looking for positivity, making the most of a different way of living, but to witness, albeit on film, a real consequence of Covid restrictions was heart-breaking. We read of operations and procedures being cancelled, but to see first-hand the repercussions, and to imagine the significance of these postponements, is sobering.

Because of the film, more people will know about Lipoedema, and how it can affect people, and most importantly that weight and body shape is not always self-inflicted. The film shows how every day, strength of character and bravery is required to overcome and manage such a condition, but to tell the story which needed to be told, required exceptional bravery, from Lorna, her family and her brother the filmmaker.

We can only hope that as vaccinations continue, and the virus becomes under control, that soon a space for an operation will become available, and that in the future we will see Lorna walking down the village, that she will be able to continue teaching children, go camping at Holm, and that one day she will dance with her children at a music festival.

Friday 22nd January

First taste of Burns became a test of character

Possibly one of the most embarrassing circumstances I have found myself in, was over 30 years ago at a Cancer Research Burns' Supper in a certain well-known Skye hotel. As a newcomer incomer to Skye, I had been taken there as part of my cultural education, to meet the good and the great, and hopefully have the craic.

The situation arose because I didn't eat meat, I still don't, not for any moral or health reason, it was only that on one day, in my late teens I stopped and never started again. When my future mother-in-law discovered my leanings she opined with certain Highland pragmatism, 'Goodness me, if we didn't eat sheep we'd be overrun with them'.

Sitting in the hotel function room with 50 or 60 other folk, instead of some nut roast or suitably subtle vegetarian haggis-like concoction, I was presented with a huge, very beautifully arranged salad. It was like an offering from outside a Buddhist temple, a kaleidoscope of sliced carrot and lettuce, without a neap or tattie in sight. The plate, which was also twice the size of any other, pointed like a neon strip light sign to me and my idiosyncrasy, reinforced by the waiter shouting out, 'Which one's the veggie?'

The wished-for hole to swallow me up never appeared, so I swallowed the salad up as quickly as possible, not due to any hunger, but purely to get it out of sight. Back in the day, I was used to being the only vegetarian at an event, but it didn't usually become a test of character, as I became the target of good-humoured comment and joke.

But there were toasts, speeches, drink and dancing, and the highlight, which in some way made up for my discomfort at the meal, was 'The Immortal Memory' given by Callum MacSween, who then taught English at the high school.

His premise was that Burns, a great poet could and should also be a conduit into other Scottish writers and wordsmiths mentioning, Norman MacCaig and of course Sorley Maclean.

The first ever Burns' night was held by a group of friends just a few years after his death, and was remarkably similar to the format which is current today, with speeches, readings, haggis and whisky. I suspect there was no lettuce eaten on that initial evening.

Burns' clubs sprang up around Ayrshire and spread, most notably abroad. Ex-pat Scots often using the event to remember homeland, and the evening now honours Scottishness as much as the bard. Coming in the sometime gloom of January, it is akin to a wedding, and although the couple have been replaced by a dead poet, there are toasts to lassies with their replies, and a celebration of relationships and romance, camaraderie and craic.

Burns seemed to like his relationships and had affairs and lovers, as well as a wife, having numerous children with at least four of these liaisons. His most well-known romantic poem however came ironically from his experience of unrequited love to Agnes Nancy Maclehose, with whom his relationship was seemingly platonic, as she was married and refused his physical advances...

Like events in a modern-day Netflix series, she left for Jamaica to try and rekindle her own marriage, but her parting from Burns inspired 'Ae fond Kiss', and some of the most beautiful words penned in love.

Had we never lov'd sae kindly,
Had we never lov'd sae blindly,
Never met-or never parted,
We had ne'er been broken-hearted.

The further irony is that the poor woman arrived in Jamaica to find her place taken by a 'slave mistress' and she eventually returned to Scotland alone. By then Burns was married to Jean Armour.

But Burns was also a radical. His upbringing had been poor, as the son of a struggling farmer, but he was educated, and schooled in Latin French and arithmetic, as well has being taught history and geography by his father. This background of tenant farming and toil may have seeded his future revolutionary political beliefs.

It is well known that Burns worked as a tax collector, but what is less noted is that his employers, the Excise Board, conducted investigations, thinking him a 'person disaffected to government' and therefore not fit and proper to be in their employment. He was spied upon and it is said he was not far from being accused and tried for sedition.

There are many less famous poems that reflect his egalitarian views on society, but 'A Man's A Man for A'That', is practically a treatise on the lot of the worker, and his views on the aristocracy seem blatant when he wrote,

Ye see yon birkie, ca'd a lord,
Wha struts, an' stares, an' a' that;
Tho' hundreds worship at his word,
He's but a coof for a' that:

The Treaty of Union between the Scottish and English Parliaments was 50 years before his birth, but his views on this political partnership and the creation of Great Britain is evident when he wrote, 'We were bought and sold for English gold, Such a parcel of rogues in a nation'. It seems likely that if he had been alive in these times, he would have been pro-independence.

It is clear to me, he was a genius, worthy of celebration due to the poetry and songs he produced, his classic works which we all know the titles of, are worth investigating and reading in full. He had flaws without doubt, and perhaps this is also why we are comfortable with celebrating him.

Poetry, like many other artistic creations, is a window on the world. It can transmit emotion and understanding, examine concepts, entertain, delight, inspire, annoy, and sometimes confuse. Above all it makes people think. There are plenty other poets out there and it is worth returning to Callum MacSween's suggestion that we can also use Burns as inspiration to find other poets, other artists.

This weekend there will be plenty of on-line virtual

Burns' nights, poems will be read out, songs sung, relationships and craic nourished. Haggis will be cooked and hopefully addressed, if only by families round the kitchen table.

And the best thing is, vegetarian haggis is now readily available.

Friday 29th January

Run, jump, slide and skid – let the urge take hold

I was about twelve or thirteen the first time I ever experienced a real whiteout in the mountains, when the snow and the mist and the land merge into a blanket of flat light almost as visually impenetrable as total darkness. Occasionally shapes loom from this optical soup, but scale is confusing and what seems to be a large crag some distance away, might be a small rock close by. The light can be a shade of pink, grey, brown, or indeed white. Once in an orange haze when skiing I fell off a six-foot drop. I couldn't make out the difference between the floor and the snow and the sky.

As a boy, most weekends I was dragged up a mountain by my parents, whatever the weather, and snow made no exception. For a youngster, it made the walks more of an adventure, more bearable and this particularday we had ventured into Great Langdale in the English Lake District not too far from where we lived. The plan was probably to ascend one of the 'Langdale Pikes', I can't recall if we made it to the top or not.

I can remember that it didn't stop snowing.

We were descending and following a compass bearing

as the mist and the snow got thicker and thicker, and the footpath had disappeared. Dad had vast hill-walking and climbing experience and the whiteout didn't put him up or down, he was happy leading the way, wading through the deep snow, breaking a path for his family in tow. Suddenly he stopped, turned around and quietly said, 'I think we should retrace our steps, just head on back the way we came, follow the footprints.' After about 30 Metres or so, the ground rose slightly, and Dad told us we could stop.

It was only then that he admitted he had accidently led us a good distance across a small lake known as 'Stickle Tarn', obviously frozen and covered with a deep layer of snow. There was no way of knowing how thick the ice was and people can die falling through ice. Dad only realised our dangerous predicament when he noticed the terrain had become unusually flat, too flat. This was the only time I ever saw him look concerned when in the mountains.

A little visibility returned and we easily followed the edge of the tarn to the stream and the way down to the valley floor where the adventures continued as our car had to be towed up a hill through deep snow by a tractor.

Snow changes things, it can turn an easy hill walk into an arctic adventure, reducing safety margins and perhaps adding risk, but it can also turn a landscape into a breathtaking wonderland, and to be immersed in a changed place can be awe-inspiring.

This weekend, Trotternish became somewhere else, blessed with blue sky, sunshine and snow. It was wonderful. We didn't need to venture far after delving into the attic to find my parents' old cross-country skis which I had purloined years ago, and a simple jaunt along the Quiriang road became a Nordic adventure.

Not only does snow change the way things look, but so often it changes our attitude. If the sun shines on white snow, it is better than any day in the summer.

There was a snowman challenge in the North end with efforts posted on social media. Prizes have yet to be awarded, but there were pipers, skiers and a Bernie Sanders complete with chair, mask, and mittens. One showed political allegiance with an old 'Yes' t-shirt, and a yacht which winters in a garden had a snow crew of three sitting on the starboard side, ready for a gust of wind. A huge traditional fellow appeared at the entrance to the primary school, reminding us that children are meant to be playing in the snow-covered playgrounds.

As many of the snowmen were made by adults as youngsters, or maybe they were all made by youngsters, it is just that some youngsters are a little older...

It seems that snow legitimises having fun and brings out the inner child which residing in everybody, reminding us that you can't beat flying out of control on a plastic sledge down the croft and that it is almost impossible not to make a snowball and throw it at the person who will make the most noise when it hits.

Seeing things differently, acting differently is always healthy, and the urge to run, jump, slide, skid and play in the snow is there in most folk.

It is always slightly manic in this household because snow-days are not that common, and we have to make the most of them, but taking opportunities is the lesson we have to take from these rare perfect days. It is always easier not to pull on the wellies and search for the sledge at the back of the shed, but as long as you don't actually hit the barbed wire fence at the bottom of the hill, it is always worth it.

Taking opportunities is also one thing I think Covid has taught us and we have to do what we can. Having studied the guidelines, it seems that under 12's can meet outdoors to engage in non-contact sport with two adult coaches or instructors. Sport Scotland supports this guideline by offering a straightforward simple online 'Covid Officers' course which is free and helps ensure that suitable protocols are in place.

This Monday, Whitewave took six local youngsters to Rubha Hunis for a 'Pandemic Picnic'. Parents dropped the kids off, in a socially distanced manner, at the start of the walk, and returned two hours later. The children got to be with their friends, and run and talk and be outside. In the spirit of home schooling and outdoor learning, we looked at some maps and discussed grid references, but most importantly we had a picnic in a beautiful place and enjoyed each other's company, in real life and not on screen.

I wonder why the various agencies and authorities don't appear to be offering outdoor recreation, and outdoor learning in small groups. It is allowed, and utterly appropriate to help with the health and well-being of our young folk. Too often we look for reasons not to do things rather than reasons to do them. Building snowmen and sledging on the croft reminds us to take opportunities, and also to make the best of the grey days as well as the perfect days, because so much is possible.

Friday 5th February

Turning athletic skill and passion into real entertainment

By chance, I was in Edinburgh on the day of the start of a stage of the 2015 'Tour of Britain' road cycling race. I was with my son who was then 13, so early in the morning, we jumped on our mountain bikes and headed to watch the spectacle at Holyrood Park.

Bradley Wiggins et al whizzed by before they headed up the Royal Mile then out south to the Borders, it wasn't as busy as I expected, and once it was all over people dissipated quickly, so we rode the few yards to the Scottish Parliament, where Ronan began jumping his bike down a series of steps, then hopping back up them.

As I was watching, I noticed two policemen also watching, one of whom was slightly incongruous in dress uniform, with lots of gold on his cap, presumably a 'top-ranker' having done a bit of civic duty at the start of the race. The other was more familiarly dressed with a tactical waistcoat and the paraphernalia of a constable on the beat.

I walked with my bicycle towards them, and gesticulated over to my son who was now wheelie-ing across the flagstones, planning another jump; 'Ermm is that ok?' I hesitantly enquired. 'Doesn't bother me', replied the man with the braid, 'As long as he's careful and doesn't cause an accident.'

I have always been convinced that it is another Skye cyclist, a certain Danny MacAskill, who helped legitimise riding bikes where they weren't intended, and turning what some used to consider anti-social behaviour and mucking about, into a recognised skill, an art form and something to be admired.

The policemen wandered off, and Ronan carried on attempting stunts.

Danny MacAskill's first video which launched his You Tube career begins with him attempting to ride across the top of some railings after jumping a few feet onto a large metal cabinet. The film focuses on the 'Danger of Death' notice stuck on the cabinet door and then to Danny who falls off a couple of times and has to bend a bit of his bike back by hitting it with a piece of wood. The message is most definitely 'keep trying'.

This is the pre-amble as after he masters the railings, the film shows him dancing his bicycle through backflips, across blocks and bollards, over barriers and along walls, using familiar Edinburgh streets and buildings as an assault course and playground.

His skills are outstanding and entertaining, obviously the result of hours and hours, over years and years of practice, but the bit in the film that stuck with me wasn't the backflip from the tree, or the jump from the flat roof of the bike shop where he used to work, it was when he replaced the car park barrier back in its holder after he had used it as a riding prop.

Here is a man that puts things back and shows respect for the street furniture that he dances on. A man from Skye that has been brought up right, and we hope that this respect has spread through to his fans and imitators. Young would-be stunt riders, might remember that it is best not to annoy, and hopefully emulate Danny's smile and politeness.

Danny brought his 'Drop and Roll' show to the Skye Agricultural Show a few years ago, and as well as the stage show stunts from scaffold towers and wooden ramps, he had an amazing jump-off with his colleague, Duncan Shaw. Youngsters crowded round cheering and shouting and there was to be a prize for whoever shouted the most from the audience.

What made me smile was the totally appropriate prize of a bike helmet. Danny might never say 'don't try this at home' but I think he would always advocate wearing a helmet. I suspect that evening there were a few ramps and jumps built on Skye crofts and driveways, with skint knees and the odd twisted handlebar following.

Danny has turned his athletic skill and passion into real entertainment and has deservedly become a worldwide video phenomenon. Alongside the awe-inspiring stunts there is humility as well as a sense of fun and humour.

One of his most popular films is entitled 'Danny's Day Care' where he pretends to baby-sit Daisy, his friend's toddler. On spotting the bike child trailer in the garden, he takes her for a hilarious and bumpy spin…

The trailer is bounced over jumps and along bridge parapets and down rough mountain bike trails on the way to the park to feed ducks and eat ice cream. We are reassured to meet Daisy's stand in stunt double doll as the credits roll after Danny amusingly fails to plait the real toddler's hair. He can balance a bicycle on its front wheel on top of a two-inch-wide metal fence, but cannot twist a hair bobble...

We also see the numerous failed attempts at the somersault off a big jump and a nod to Danny's most well-known video when he pretends to take her up the inaccessible Pinnacle in the Cuillin mountains on Skye.

The Ridge has had over 74 million views, it is audacious and breath taking and made more beautiful by the use of Martyn Bennet's adaptation of Lizzie Higgins singing 'Blackbird' from the album 'Grit'. When this inspirational tune was chosen, I am sure they would never have guessed that it would lead to a theatrical performance at Celtic Connections where aspects of the film were recreated on stage during an orchestral performance of Bennet's music.

As an example of audience development, it was a stroke of genius. Bike fans got to hear and see an amazing orchestral show, and music fans got to experience some live bike trick riding.

Danny is possibly Skye's most famous son at the moment, and it is well deserved. He is talented and an appropriate entertainer, a great 'Drop and Roll' model to inspire young folk who want to follow their passion. His latest film 'The Slabs' has just been released, in it he descends the 'Dubh Slabs' in the Cuillins. Find it on You Tube, although you might end up biting your fingernails while watching it.

Friday 12 February

We are taught, but only from our own mistakes do we learn

It was one of the last sessions on my degree course, and the lecturer had asked us to take something into class connected with the outdoors to use as a basis for a talk. It was really an end-of-term winding down get together, allowing each of us to tell a story. I took a photograph of an incredible cave I had visited, possibly one of the most beautiful places I have been, filled with delicate pure white straw stalactites many feet long, its beauty was made more so by the cavern's inaccessibility. It was horrible to get to it.

However, another colleague brought a very small rock, and allowed us look at it, touch it, feel it. It was light in colour and had edges. A piece of limestone that had not been worn down by the elements, geologically young as a mere 470 million years ago this particular stone would have been part of the sea floor, being formed from the shells of marine invertebrates, living creatures.

The earth's tectonic plates, floating on a sea of magma, can sometimes push together and the seabed can rise and become a mountain range. The piece of seabed we held that day had indeed risen, my friend had picked it up from near the top of Everest.

The highest places on the planet used to be at the bottom of the sea, and they are still growing. It has been suggested that the height is increasing by just over 1 millimetre a year which might not sound very much, but in a million-years' time, a mere blink of an eye in the age of the earth, Everest might grow by over a kilometre, as if it's not big enough already.

Geology was only part of my friend's story. He was an experienced Himalayan mountaineer and had been on several expeditions to Everest. One time he was over 8000 metres high, but it was quite late in the day and there was the possibility of worsening weather. Although within striking distance of the summit, he made the decision not to risk going further and retreated, after picking up a small piece of the mountain and putting it in his pocket.

Last Friday we turned back on one of our trig point walks. Anne had had an appointment in Broadford so afterwards we took the opportunity to venture further afield and explore the south end. Sgurr na Coinnich is no Everest but is a sizable hill on the way to Kylerhea. Being older than the Himalayan mountains, it may have grown some, but has been worn down over millennia by ice, wind and rain to a more achievable level for most.

The top 1000 feet were still well clad with snow and although the ground was not too steep, at one point while traversing a slope Anne asked casually, 'This wouldn't avalanche, would it?' As I replied in the negative saying, 'It's not steep enough' two things happened. First of all there was a weird creaking vibration that could be felt through and from the snow which was beginning to groan and feel like a floating slab on a not very solid base, and secondly, I looked down and realised that I actually had no idea how steep a slope had to be before it might avalanche...

It was only a few steps to solid tussocky ground, but avalanche risk or not, I was beginning to feel like we should have had ice axes as a slip would result in quite a long slide. Although the days are stretching, it would also have been good to have been a couple of hours earlier in the day and it was only going to get colder.

I have always considered risk in the outdoors a bit like lemons in a slot machine. 5 in a row and you might end up having an epic, we were perhaps at 2.

Carrying on to a small bealach on a ridge, we had our egg sandwiches and considered it the high point for the day. The creaking snow slope could be avoided on our descent, and it wasn't long before we reached flatter terrain thus reducing the lemon count.

I have since discovered that slab avalanches can occur on slopes as shallow as 25 degrees, and are most common between 30 and 45 degrees, I reckon the slope that creaked was between 30 and 45 degrees. It wasn't a big snowfield, and not far to the gentler aspect below, but who knows what might have happened if we had triggered even a small slide.

It has been said only partly in jest, that good practice comes from experience, but experience comes from bad practice. We learn from mistakes, close calls, near misses. With all the training and teaching of skills that is available nowadays, there is no excuse for bad practice, but in all reality, despite the sense of learning from the practice of other people, it is only when putting recent teaching into our own practice, away from a guide or an instructor that most lessons are learnt.

I have no idea if the slope we were on could have avalanched, but the experience has reminded me that the mountains in winter are very different to summer. Snow and ice add a layer of beauty and change which inspires exploration but also adds a layer of risk. Winter can be unforgiving in the mountains.

It is positive to expand our comfort zones, relearn forgotten skills, and gain new, so on returning home it took all of ten minutes to order two modern lightweight ice axes from an online supplier, his and hers.

When they arrive, we shall be throwing ourselves down safe concave snow slopes, practicing how to brake with the axe, it is simple enough, but like everything needs practice.

I shall also read up on recognising avalanche conditions...

But perhaps one of the most important skills is to know when enough is enough, and when to turn back. My friend never got another attempt on Everest, but his small rock I found inspirational as a totem for sensible decision making. Anne and I can return to Sgurr na Coinnich anytime. It is not going away.

The Scottish Avalanche Information Service does not cover Skye but gives information for other mountain areas. The organisation provides a 'Be Avalanche Aware' app which is free to download.

Friday 19th February

Relief at the rain as 'controlled burning' gets out of hand

The first time I was in Australia was nearly fifteen years ago, Anne had been singing at the Woodford festival in Queensland, after which we flew south to Melbourne. On exiting the airport, we were hit by a woody smoky smell and an accompanying haze. Bush fires had been going for some time and although the burning was a long way from the city, depending on wind direction and intensity, there was a marked effect on air quality. Some days were worse than others but folk were getting fed up of a constant cloying atmosphere.

Driving north to a small festival at Daylesford, we took the opportunity to explore a national park which had burned the year before. In places the ground was quite barren but through blackened earth were unmistakable signs of nature returning. Green saplings were pushing through and there was already a lot of reedy grass. Some trees had survived and were in leaf again, and to the delight of my kids, a mob of wallabies bounded close by, leaping over charcoaled branches and through the new undergrowth.

A pyrophytic plant is one that has adapted to survive fire,

indeed some even require fire to germinate. Resin-coated seeds need a flame to melt the case and allow growth, and some require chemicals from ash to break their dormancy in the ground. Quick growing species take advantage of space created by fire, while certain gum trees have adapted to re-sprout when branches and buds are lost by burning. Other plants have developed a system of fire insulation with layers of dead leaves protecting their stems.

In Tasmania we witnessed a bush fire perhaps too closely, having been stopped by fire fighters and their trucks who advised us not to continue driving on, although reassuring us that it was safe enough to stay and watch the helicopter dousing flames some distance away using a big bucket of water suspended beneath, refilled from a dam close by.

Most of the villages and towns displayed fire danger rating signs, a pointer could be moved from green (low to medium risk) through blue to yellow orange and red (high, severe and extreme). There were many reminders of the total fire ban.

Last year the Australian bush fires were worse than ever, and their impacts were making world news. Anne had been invited to sing at a small festival in Victoria and our plan was to extend the trip into a holiday. But as the fires raged, a number of music festivals were cancelled, and travel in certain areas was either banned or discouraged. In the weeks and days running up to our departure date, we watched the news closely, and were in regular contact with the festival organisers and the cousins we hoped to visit.

The fires were however in other areas and seemingly the festival would run, the consensus was that we should go, indeed, spend our money as the tourist industry was taking a hit all over.

As it happened, our trip went off without a hitch and the only evidence we saw of fires was when walking in the Victorian Alps, but the main impact was empty villages, bereft of visitors. Many of the shops, bars and cafes had chalk boards and signs outside stating they were open, almost pleading for trade...

Like a premonition of Covid times to come.

An unprecedented 110,000 square kilometres were burnt that summer. Many people lost their homes and livelihoods and over thirty people tragically lost their lives, including four firefighters.

The reason the fires were so intense has been put down to drought conditions, unusually high temperatures and strong winds, and also the thought that undergrowth was denser creating more fuel for the fires.

The indigenous peoples of Australia used to deliberately burn the bush, managing areas to allow a more diverse species growth and help with hunter-gathering. It also helped prevent massive fires. In 2002 the Australian Parliament discussed recommendations that similar management fires be used as a tool to reduce the fuel loading in a forest.

Fighting fire with fire.

A number of my friends and neighbours here on Skye are firefighters and some I know were relieved when it rained this weekend. Some of the heather and grass fires of late had been getting out of hand. The concept of 'controlled burning' is perhaps an elastic one.

I have always known this burning to be called a falaisgear

and thought that the phrase 'muir burning' was more specific to grouse moor strip burning, but it seems that the Scots word is becoming common parlance here on the west, perhaps due to its use in legal terminology and suggested guidelines.

Whatever it is called, it is contentious, almost as divisive as recent referenda. It is possible that land management issues should be added to religion and politics as subjects to be avoided in polite company...

Burning old-growth heather and matted dead grass as a way of encouraging new growth for grazing is a recognised appropriate land management technique. It does however have to be done safely and within parameters. Controlled burning.

The later in the year, the worse it is for ground nesting birds; hence the cut-off point of April 15. A healthy meadow pipit and skylark population is as important as well-fed sheep. Debate as to the negative environmental impact of falaisgear will rage as fiercely as some of the fires which burnt last week, although 'Nature Scotland' (formally SNH) the agency tasked with looking after our natural heritage, states that, 'Fire is one of our oldest and most powerful land management tools'. Their biggest environmental concern seems to be the risk of fire getting into and damaging deep peat.

I have heard that in years gone by, a falaisgear was more of a community event, more people around to keep an eye on it and protect the fences. Perhaps more regular burning made for less fuel loading, and smaller fires. Perhaps when they got out of hand fewer people noticed.

A friend of mine was driving home last week and was almost engulfed by fire.

She was terrified.

Perhaps it is time for landowners, crofters, gamekeepers, estate managers, fire and rescue services and environmental agencies to not only get around a table and talk, but also manufacture a way of sharing or gaining practical experience. 'Nature Scotland' also states that burning 'requires planning, skill and experience.' This skill and experience has to come from somewhere.

Friday 26th February

As simple and powerful as flicking a switch

There was a light switch at the bottom of our stairs, it turned the upstairs landing light on or off. There was another switch at the entrance to my parents' bedroom, which turned the same light on or off. What always confused me, as a small boy, was that operating each switch regardless of whether it was up or down, would have the result of turning the light on if it was off or off if it was already on. The opposite of what the light was doing at the time.

At some stage, a rudimentary electronics experiments kit arrived at the house, I don't remember if it was mine or my older brother's, but it was one of those educational toys occasionally bought by well-meaning parents, hoping some useful knowledge will rub off on their offspring.

Crude circuits could be made by attaching wires to springs, batteries and bulbs, I think there was even a small speaker and a way of producing beeps. There was definitely a switch.

I understood the concept of a switch breaking or connecting a circuit, like a drawbridge over a river, but it didn't help with the matter of our upstairs light. I was still mystified as to how the same action could have either result, how flicking the switch down could both turn the light on or off.

It was only years later when I was renovating our first little house in Idrigill that the mystery was solved. There is an extra wire, and each switch can break one circuit, but makes the possibility of a parallel circuit which can be connected or not at the other end.

Switches are powerful things, and completely fundamental to modern living, and not just by throwing light on the way to the toilet at night.

On a very basic and simplified level, a computer is full of millions of switches, and as they were developed, so too was a standardised code which could represent language, and eventually sound and images by a code of ones or zeros, which in turn can be stored and processed by electrical signals.

On or off switches.

The first computers contained physical switches, and consequently were huge, my father was an accountant for local government, and in the 1960's he oversaw the modernising of his department. The first computer had to be craned in through the roof. The phone in my pocket will have considerably more computing power than this early machine that filled a room. Dad would bring home used punch cards and what we called computer paper, with rows of holes each side to allow it to feed into the machine. We used it for drawing on.

As I understand it, the screen I am looking at now has thousands of pixels, chunks, a grid. Every pixel has the ability to change colour, and as each colour has a code, a series of ones or zeros, the colour of the pixels can be controlled or stored by switches. The same goes for music.

It is as simple as it is complicated.

But these switches do more than store pictures, language and sound, they can process them by following instructions. A computer program is like a very complicated flow diagram. If X happens do Y, if W happens do Y then Z, all processes can be broken down into very long pathways of what is known as a binary choice. Yes or no. On or off.

These instructions are also known as algorithms, and exist in all aspects of our digital lives.

It has been suggested to me that when Donald Trump was banned from Twitter it probably happened automatically, the computers controlling the social media platform perhaps recognising the use of certain words, which when repeated, set into process a series of events culminating in the closing of the account. Perhaps such a high-profile account as a President of the USA will have had more human intervention, but monitoring accounts is part and parcel of what these platforms do, and it has to be done by computer. There is just so much data.

It is probably safe to say that the real reason social media and our internet use is monitored is commerciality, and that any overseeing of morality, or issue such as hate crime, is possibly more a useful by-product.

The corporations are far more interested in us as both potential customers, and the data about our behaviour which is in itself hard currency. Algorithms control this. If I click on an internet site selling motorbike tyres, it isn't long before I start receiving adverts for motorbike tyres, and indeed all aspects of motorcycles. When I got to a certain age, I started receiving retirement plan portfolio adverts (chance would be a fine thing). In this digital age, we are the product, and if it frustrates us, I guess we have to see it as the price to pay for a 'free' service. These companies, rich as they might be, have to make money, their computers, programmers, analysts, marketers, offices all need paid for, as well as making a profit.

What is perhaps more insidious is the manipulation of our virtual social life, in the same way that the platforms recognise my spending habits, they also recognise my political and wider curiosities and likes, and the people I interact with online. All controlled through algorithms. Those operating the platforms would likely argue that they are providing a valuable service, moulding the content of our internet to suit us, personalising our devices. What it is also doing is creating something called an 'echo chamber' an environment in which a person encounters only beliefs or opinions that coincide with their own, so that their existing views are reinforced and alternative ideas are perhaps not considered.

Society needs debate, it needs healthy respectful argument and we need to constantly be aware of different opinion, other ways of doing. However, there is a danger that we are being manipulated into polarised dogmatic encampments, and it is as much the result of algorithmic social media platforms, as any other media or process.

Whilst the power and ability of computers is developing at an incredible rate, the consequence to society is perhaps not yet fully understood.

We should remember it is just a series of switches and maybe occasionally we should turn them off.

Chapter Seven

March 2021

Understanding semiotics – a sign of the times / A salute to the women who have faced a steeper climb/ Covid Kids' experience can change our schools / Even in the most difficult times, there is always good news

Friday 5th March

Understanding semiotics – a sign of the times

I am old enough and lucky enough to have received a sizable student grant when first going to college, means-tested and appropriately topped up by the parents. It was a rite of passage when leaving home for the first time, to immediately visit a hi-fi shop and put a less appropriate, but satisfying dent in the new bank account, and return to the student accommodation or rented flat with the biggest speakers, and most extravagant stereo system one could not really justify.

It seems that now students just have their phones, and an online streaming platform, connected via Bluetooth to a small but powerful speaker with a built-in amplifier. The quality is not that of our old vinyl-driven racked up monoliths, but it's not half bad, and they are a lot easier to carry about, there is however a reason that originally speakers were called loudspeakers...

I came across my original amplifier in the attic the other day, bought with that first grant cheque, the original speakers are in my kitchen, nearly 40 years old and still producing sound. The amplifier sadly started distorting and after various buttons stopped working and the volume control became more like an on-off switch, it was retired, which of course means being kept in the attic for years.

Still 'blu-tacked' to the volume dial is a CND button badge, next to a small sticker of a whale above the 'Technics' nameplate.

The CND logo is possibly one of the most recognisable, ubiquitous symbols in existence. Back in the day the stickers practically came with an offer of a university place, gracing our guitar cases, sometimes our guitars. If folk managed to get to the dizzying heights of owning a car, they would be stuck on the back windscreen. Files and folders, bags and lapels, it was a sign that you were a student, and we kidded ourselves that alongside the Greenpeace and Amnesty International stickers, it signified a socially minded bohemian cool.

I only discovered recently that the CND 'peace' symbol was designed by a British artist Gerald Holtom in 1958. His original ideas incorporated the Christian cross within a circle, but it was felt by original members of the inaugural London CND meeting, that a cross would have 'too many wrong associations', so the arms took a turn downwards.

It is said that the inspiration for this move came from semaphore flag signaling, combining the signs representing N for nuclear and D for disarmament.

The logo was never trademarked, and has become the internationally understood symbol for peace, over and above the original campaign against nuclear weapons.

Semaphore was an original communication system of a fighting navy ship, and apparently is still understood and used presumably as a back-up in certain manoeuvres. There is a pleasing irony that naval communication and symbolism was part of the creative process in the placards that still adorn the peace camp at Faslane!

Signs, symbols and logos are a huge part of communication, many commercial designs are instantly recognisable by most. The apple with a bite (or byte!) taken from it on my laptop, the three stripes, or curved flash on trainers and running shoes, the four interlocking circles on my neighbour's car and the number 57 on the can of beans in my kitchen cupboard. All immediately recognisable.

Semiotics, at its simplest, means the study of signs. It gets more complicated when we realise that signs are more than just logos for commercial companies or social organisations, and more than just information to do with road safety and navigation or the symbols for apps on our phones.

Signs are everywhere, they can be visual, auditory, linguistic, and include context and culture. Signs have to be decoded by the receiver, which is a learnt skill.

In the West, if we shake our head from side to side, it generally means 'No', in India, shaking the head can mean a multitude of things, and often means 'yes' or 'I understand'. Much of meaning comes from context, and it is the sort of visual sign that semioticians love studying.

Non-verbal communication is semiotics in action. A shrug, a roll of the eyes, looking away, thousands of subtle and less subtle movements are all signs that either replace, emphasise or belie language.

Occasionally when I am working with youth groups, we talk about listening and communicating, and in the middle of a session, I have been known to go and sit on the floor at the edge of the group, play acting, slumped with my head in my hands. After not speaking for a while, I ask the youngsters, what am I communicating?

They very quickly catch on that my behaviour might be because of, being upset, being bullied, disengagement or just boredom, any number of things. Communicated by what we call body language, not necessarily vocalised, but often generally understood.

Although we are becoming used to the two dimensions of screen communication, perhaps we should endeavour to look for the subtleties of body language. Constantly we only see the head and shoulders of our friends, families and work colleagues and extra signs may be masked as folk stare squarely at the screen. Non-verbal messaging is not as obvious in a gallery of boxes, and perhaps not as easy to read.

Nuances of language also becomes more important, as it is vital that we keep an eye on the well-being of the people we only see virtually, and this might require more sensitivity to the signs, codes and communication given out. Remember the word 'Fine', a word that can mean nothing or everything, the whole continuum of emotion from despair to elation. Rather like the Indian head wobble, it is all about context, but with only a digital box, the full picture may be difficult to ascertain.

Semiotically speaking, we have all learnt new language, new signs, in conjunction with our changed existence, but yesterday I saw the best sign yet. A wooden half barrel full of purple flowering crocuses. A sign that someone wants to add colour to the world, and a sign of spring.

Friday 12th March

A salute to the women who have faced a steeper climb

In 2015 I was invited to speak at the Himalayan Mountain Writer's Festival, held in Musoorie, Uttarakhand, Northern India. On discovering that the theme was 'Women & Mountains' one of my friends immediately quipped that he wasn't sure which I knew least about... As they had offered to fly me out and look after me, I wasn't going to let this aspersion get in my way.

It was mainly a literary event, but I had been asked to tell the story of Whitewave, as a nod to the theme I interspersed my tale with books that I have found inspirational over the years and also began my talk with a picture of an amazing young woman.

She is leaning on a metal bollard at the junction of a road in a mountain village. The image is black and white, probably taken in the mid 1950's. Her woolen bobble hat wouldn't look out of place on a youngster today, and I could imagine my son wearing her 'Ventile' cotton smock while snowboarding.

More indicative of the era are the thick corduroy trousers tucked into nailed leather boots and the hawser-laid climbing rope coiled and slung over her shoulder. She looks every inch what used to be called a 'tomboy' and has the hint of a posed smile, gazing up at the mountain and crags she hopes to climb later.

The picture is of my mother.

Only recently I discovered that it was she who bought the climbing rope, and not my father, she who insisted they move from the easy scrambles to the more precipitous faces requiring rope, and well just a rope in those days. No harness or belay devices, no metal nuts or camming protection for the lead climber, and no helmets. Just a thin rope tied with a bowline around your waist. It didn't do to actually fall off.

She was by no means the first, or best woman climber, and didn't claim any tough first ascents or push boundaries, but she climbed, and told me she loved the feeling of her hands on warm dry rock as she pulled herself up climbs mainly in North Wales, but occasionally here on Skye.

It certainly wasn't common for women to climb, so in some respects perhaps she was a pioneer, helping pave the way for women to have more choice in how they spend their time. Normalising adventure for women.

March the 8th is International Women's Day, a global day celebrating the social, economic, cultural and political achievements of women. The day also intends to raise awareness and hopes to accelerate gender parity.

A lot has changed in the 65 years since the photograph was taken of my mother, but still there are barriers and low ceilings in society preventing the total emancipation of women. The organisers of International Women's Day suggest that real gender parity will not come about in our lifetime. The theme for this year is 'Choose to Challenge' as they suggest a challenged world is an alert world.

Dr Danielle Stewart was interviewed on Radio Scotland as part of the day's celebrations. 'Highly commended' in this years 'Top 50 Women in Engineering', she is the long-term strategy manager for the National Grid. Her doctorate was in Particle Physics.

She told of often being in the minority in a room and feeling like 'the other', often the only female in a department or meeting but insisting that the key 'Is to trust that you are credible and deserve to be there.'

Dr Stewart also said we have to question perceptions. Occasionally people would phone, having assumed that Dr Stewart was a man they would think that they had the wrong number when she answered.

Not just in engineering.

On one occasion at Whitewave, a couple had booked in for a kayaking session, I led them up to the meeting room where I introduced them to Gillian, the woman who would be taking them out. Although we stood in a small circle, the gentleman insisted on directing all his questions to me, his body language blanking out our instructor as he turned just slightly, to face me. Eventually I had to make my excuses and walked away so they would direct their questions to their instructor.

Of course, it was a great session, and afterwards, when the clients had gone, we laughed about the inauspicious beginning... sort of. We also talked at length about what was going on in that initial meeting.

Of course, women work in the outdoors, but they are still

in the minority, they recreate in the outdoors, but are still in the minority.

Mollie Hughes is the youngest woman to have climbed Everest, reaching the summit in 2012 at the age of 26. Five years later she summitted a second time. She was also interviewed on radio this week and when asked how many other women were on the mountain on expeditions, she estimated about 1 in 10 climbers were female.

It could perhaps be argued that it is more important that society works towards more female engineers than climbers, but role models, attitudes and perceptions should all be carefully examined and probably challenged. Crucially, any girl who wants to be an engineer, or outdoor instructor, or Himalayan mountain climber, should have the same opportunity as any boy. To do likewise.

My mother never spoke of being unusual, or mentioned any barriers to her wanting to climb, and although a primary school teacher, on the birth of my brother and then me, she perhaps ironically played a very traditional housewife and mother role – although dragged her family to the hills at every opportunity.

Speaking before me at the Himalayan festival, was Gerlinde Kaltenbrunner, the first woman to climb all 14 mountains over 8000 metres without supplemental oxygen breathing apparatus. She spoke movingly and received huge applause as she told of reaching the top of K2, her final top.

To say I was nervous 'following that' with a tale of a wee outdoor centre in the north of Skye, would be an understatement.

The picture of my Mum won the day.

Friday 19 March

Covid kids' experience can change our schools

I recently came across a picture of a stone carving, apparently situated at the entrance to George Heriot's school in Edinburgh. A group of people are sat behind a tiered desk while two others are stood out to one side. At the other side is a bearded man. The carving is over four hundred years old, so the style of dress consists of tights, robes, breeches and ruffs, and although the double row of desks is more reminiscent of a choir stall, the scene is instantly recognisable as a school classroom.

The pupils are not sat rigidly and in the relief is evidence of movement and dialogue. It also bears a Latin inscription which translates as, 'God has given us this leisure', suggesting a belief in the divine right to education.

This week sees young people in Scotland return to the school buildings they vacated last year. It seems unfair to say they are returning to school, as teachers, parents and carers have been striving to provide some form of schooling during lockdown, and the pupils themselves have had to adapt to a significantly different way of doing things, relying much more on self-motivation and direction.

Sir Ken Robinson the well-known educationalist, who sadly died of cancer last year, suggested that young people have an extraordinary capacity for innovation, and in one of his lectures told the story of an eight-year-old girl quietly drawing in the back of a classroom. The teacher walked over to ask what she was drawing, and was informed, 'I'm drawing a picture of God.' The teacher then said, 'But nobody knows what God looks like,' to be told, 'They will in a minute.'

Robinson also believed that creativity is not something that children grow into, but have educated out by school systems prioritising academic achievement and conformity rather than imagination and initiative.

One of the benefits of the pandemic has been the chance for people to re-evaluate priorities and mindset and whilst there is an obvious desire to return to a life similar to the pre-pandemic state, there is also a feeling that things could be different.

One opportunity could be to look at the way we educate our young people, and the two aspects that might be debated are the way we teach, and what we teach.

For some, home learning, a mixture of self-directed and internet-based lesson work, has been fantastic, those youngsters that can't abide distraction, and are happy to work on their own. For others it has been a disaster with no direction, no motivation and a need for a teacher to be constantly present with encouragement and explanation. For many it will have been a combination.

It is well known that there are distinct learning styles. Some people like to see, some prefer to hear, some need to read, whilst others like to be more hands on, more tactile. Many will appreciate a combination, and an experienced teacher will have techniques that encompass all styles, an holistic approach.

Addressing all these styles solely through computer and screen will have been a tough challenge, which is why for some face-to-face is imperative, but the way lessons are delivered, the way learning is frame-worked and structured, will always be a compromise, and more advantageous to some than others.

A blended approach could actually be a model we aspire to, build on and hone rather than just a temporary measure. Robinson suggested that our schools were still based on the factories they were meant to populate in the industrial revolution. Specific time periods marked by bells, batches of youngsters grouped by age, housed in departments which more often than not contain teachers imparting knowledge at the front of rows of desks or tables. Crucially, our children are minded throughout the working day, freeing up the parent or carer for employment.

John Swinney, the Cabinet Secretary for Education and Skills has repeatedly stated that schooling provides social interaction for young people, crucial to their health and well-being, and a huge factor in the need for a return to school. Whilst massively beneficial, the irony is that this interaction is really a by-product. There could easily be more effective ways of facilitating social interaction.

The young people returning to Portree High School this week might be working till 2070, if there are any jobs then, babies being born now will live to the 22nd century. We really don't have much idea what society and the world will be like by then. That technological advances will continue to accelerate, and the environment will continue to deteriorate, is probably all we can be sure of.

So what should we educate our children for?

Yuval Noah Harari, the Israeli author, writes that modern pedological experts suggest we should switch to teaching the four 'C's'; Critical thinking, Collaboration, Communication and Creativity, and emphasise general life skills, whatever they may be.

These could obviously be achieved through traditional subjects, but the emphasis would be on process rather than subject. Understanding rather than knowledge. It could be argued that facts themselves are becoming increasingly irrelevant as practically all information is just a few clicks away.

I have no fear that the Covid cohorts of scholars, who had this very different experience, will do alright. The same percentage will succeed, whatever that means, they will have the same spread of achievement or not, and will find their place in society just like those who went before. The debate might be in a few years' time, when we actually can't tell who missed a few months of traditional schooling, and then the question might well be asked. Why would we continue schooling our children in a way more akin to a stone carving in Edinburgh, than trying to create something fit for the 21st century?

If I were to start with a blank piece of paper, there would of course be traditional subjects, but also a greater emphasis on, music and the arts, philosophy, and how and why people think. There would be more outdoor learning, more residential experience, and more physical activity. Instead of being walled fortresses away from the community, our schools should be hubs for all learners. Less time would be spent in the school itself, complemented by virtual learning at home (or anywhere.)

There is also a well-known saying that is worth being mindful of, 'You don't fatten a pig by measuring it'. Perhaps we are also too obsessed with tests and examinations and their results.

Friday 16th March

Even in the most difficult times, there is always good news

It has been suggested that there are only a handful of basic plots which reoccur in most of the films, plays and books that we watch or read. Although overlapping, these plots have been simplified and explained to be either quests and voyages, the overcoming of adversity or evil, rebirth or coming of age, with either comedy or tragedy as a theme. They can of course be more nuanced, and occasionally confused with layers of sub-plot and added complexity, but on the whole the threads are basic and universal.

Stories are how we make sense of the world, they allow us to understand each other, with all our idiosyncrasies and complexities, and they allow us to share our experiences, what has happened to us, the lives that we lead.

The narrative however is something slightly different, it is how we angle our stories, how the events and experiences are retold. With a narrative comes interpretation, editing, a point of view, the idea of the story. With a different perspective, the same story can have a different narrative.

It has been exactly a year since the first lockdown in the UK, and sometimes it seems that these past twelve months might have originated from the imaginations of a team of writers creating the third season of a streamed Netflix series. Much of it wouldn't be believable if seen on the big screen, and even though we have lived through and experienced the unfolding drama, a lot still seems implausible.

This is perhaps because alongside the story, we have had a specific narrative related to us throughout the last year. It has been distilled, simplified into a basic theme of negativity.

There has been real tragedy, and we cannot and should not downplay the fact that people have died prematurely due to Covid, and there has been an increased use of food banks, some people have lost businesses, had significantly reduced income, and some key workers have been close to burnout, and some people have struggled with their mental health.

Many have just been frustrated with restrictions and guidelines.

The story could have come direct from a Hollywood movie, a virus threatening the whole population on earth. The plot is how humanity has dealt with this threat, how governments have reacted and how society has coped with the different attempts to control the pandemic.

The narrative is societies' mind-set and its interpretation of these events. Most of this comes via the media, news, whether read, watched or listened to and edited by corporation, organisation, or through the algorithms controlling our own social media. On the whole, the interpretation is out of our hands.

News almost by definition is bad. There have been

studies that suggest that in the media, bad news items outweigh good by as much as tenfold. This is obviously not that bad things outweigh good by ten, it is just what is reported, what makes the news and what the narrative is.

Also researched have been people's attitude to news, and the bad news is, that people seem to prefer bad news. There may well be a negativity bias suggesting a hunger to hear and respond to bad news. This is not just schadenfreude, a pleasure that derives from another person's misfortune, as there is the suggestion that it stems from hunter gatherer days when a survival instinct needed to concentrate on danger. It seems we might be psychologically hard wired to be more in tune to negative events, as they are the ones we had to be aware of to keep us safe.

This is now manifest in what news is reported, and now a self-perpetuating formula. Bad news makes people watch the television, and so that's what we get. Every day we hear how many people have died from the pandemic, not how many babies have been born. How many people have been hospitalised, not how many have been discharged, or how many families finally saw their granny in the care home, or held hands. Even the deaths have been reduced to statistics, so we concentrate on the passing and not the lives they led.

Sensationalist headlines will get more attention and keep people addicted to a news cycle, media outlets will concentrate on disaster reporting. It has been suggested that constant exposure to negative information can have a negative impact on mood and psyche and can lead to symptoms of fatigue, anxiety and depression.

We should not ignore the sad and the bad, but a more

balanced interpretation might help with the mental welfare of society and help us deal with grief, after all grieving is as much about celebration of life as the sadness of its passing.

A Huffington Post article suggested, 'A more positive form of journalism will not only benefit our well-being; it will engage us in society, and it will help catalyse potential solutions to the problems that we face.' We need more good news.

The puppet animation by Dominic More Gordon and produced by Young Films of Skye, has been chosen by the BBC to mark the first anniversary of lockdown in the UK. This is good news.

A wee 'Westie' runs along the hallway to collect mail which has dropped through the letter box off camera. The dog delivers the envelope to Archie, an older larger dog, sitting at the table having his breakfast. There is a short note and a key, a relative from the Outer Hebrides has died, and bequeathed her house to Archie. We follow the two felted puppet dogs on a bittersweet adventure as they journey by train and ferry through wind and rain to the tin roofed 'but and ben'.

It is a beautiful creation, both poignant and whimsical but appropriate in its simplicity and universality. By choosing an animation with no dialogue, we can make of it what we will, on any number of levels.

The plot covers both voyage and adversity, there is sadness, but joy overcomes. The final scene has both characters, stood in the doorway of the wee croft house in the sunshine, the calm that follows the storm. Perhaps it takes a short animation featuring anthropomorphic dogs to remind us of societies' positivity. This positivity however is not fiction, the world has more good in it than bad, even if that is not what is reported. Maybe we should take this lockdown anniversary to remember the losses, but also to celebrate what is good, question the narrative, and tell our own story.

Acknowledgments

My life would be incomplete without Anne Martin, who keeps me right in more ways than she could ever imagine, in addition to casting an eye over the columns each week before submission. My children who also keep me grounded but inspire me and have added to the adventure of life. Keith Mackenzie, editor of the West Highland Free Press, a paper which punches above its weight, who has allowed me the privilege of a public voice. Thanks to my brother Richard who helped tidy up the final manuscript, chasing spelling mistakes and 'Weird Wandering Apostrophes'. Thanks also to Duncan Lockerbie at Lumphanan Press for advice and design skills.

My friends and neighbours with whom I have conversations and who continue to provide inspiration, and the readers who by buying the paper support journalism, and a local business.

Lastly the people who encourage my writing by making comment. A shout out must go to the lady outside the Co-Op who made my day when telling me she enjoyed my articles. I thanked her, adding that I hoped I didn't ever offend her, she replied with a smile, 'Och I just skip over those bits.'